Management Development and Educational Reform

A HANDBOOK FOR SECONDARY SCHOOLS

AGNES McMAHON
and
RAY BOLAM

P·C·P
Paul Chapman
Publishing Ltd

Copyright © 1990 National Development Centre for
Educational Management and Policy

First published 1990

Paul Chapman Publishing Ltd
144 Liverpool Road
London
N1 1LA

British Library Cataloguing in Publication Data

McMahon, Agnes
  A handbook for secondary schools. –
  (Management development and educational reform)
  1. Great Britain. Secondary Schools. Management
  I. Title II. Bolam, Ray
  371.2′00941

ISBN 1–85396–080–2

Typeset by Inforum Typesetting, Portsmouth
Printed and bound by Butler and Tanner, Frome.

A B C D E F G 5 4 3 2 1 0

CONTENTS

FOREWORD AND ACKNOWLEDGEMENTS

There are three books on management development and educational reform in this series:

- *A Handbook for LEAs.*
- *A Handbook for Primary Schools.*
- *A Handbook for Secondary Schools.*

Many people have contributed to the production of this handbook. We are extremely grateful for the invaluable help and advice received from the head-teachers, teachers and the LEA co-ordinators in the schools and authorities that collaborated with us to work on management development. They tried out and then commented on the draft materials and also supplied many of the illustrative examples. (We have listed the LEAs and schools in Appendix II). We are also grateful to the members of the NDC Steering Committee and to Elizabeth Ballinger and Beryl Evans for their helpful advice and suggestions. We wish to thank our colleagues at the National Development Centre – Valerie Hall, David Oldroyd and Mike Wallace – for their annotated suggestions and hours of discussion. Finally, we thank June Collins, Joan Moore, Mary Purchase, Sue Queree and Angela Allen for their skill and forbearance in producing and reprocessing several drafts of the handbook while working to very tight deadlines.

Agnes McMahon
Ray Bolam
Bristol

Agnes McMahon is a Research Fellow in the School of Education at the University of Bristol. She has acted as consultant and researcher to LEAs and the DES, the Schools Council and the Training Agency, and is currently co-ordinating the Teacher Appraisal Pilot Schemes. She has published widely on teacher induction, school self-review, management development and teacher appraisal.

Ray Bolam is Director of the National Development Centre for Educational Management and Policy and of Further Professional Studies in the University of Bristol. He has acted as consultant and researcher for LEAs, the DES, OECD and for several governments. He has published widely in the field of professional development and the management of educational change.

PART I
INTRODUCTION

1
MANAGEMENT DEVELOPMENT AND EDUCATIONAL REFORM

What is the Purpose of this Handbook?

The main purpose of this handbook is to help headteachers and senior staff in secondary, middle and special schools to plan, implement and evaluate a management development policy and a programme of activities that will improve the way individuals and groups of teachers manage schools and that, in the longer term, should improve teaching and learning. Its immediate purpose is to suggest how they can build on their present practice in a reasonably systematic fashion in order to develop a coherent policy-led approach to management development.

The handbook has been produced in collaboration with headteachers, teachers and advisers from 33 secondary, middle and special schools in eight LEAs. It contains practical suggestions for action that are illustrated with examples from experience in these schools. There is an accompanying LEA handbook (McMahon and Bolam, 1990a) that suggests how an LEA can support management development for teachers across an authority.

Whom is the Handbook for?

The handbook is aimed at headteachers and teachers in secondary, middle and special schools who have a formal school management responsibility. We define school management as working with and through professional teachers and other adults in order to achieve the goals of the school. This responsibility is related to but distinct from classroom teaching and management. The handbook should, therefore, be particularly relevant to deputy headteachers, heads of department, pastoral heads, professional tutors and in-service co-ordinators as well as the headteacher. It should also be useful for members of school governing bodies.

What is Management Development?

Management development is part of staff development. Whereas a staff-development policy and programme is concerned with the development of all teachers in the school in all aspects of their role (including their classroom teaching), management development focuses mainly on those teachers who have a formal school management responsibility and upon the way they handle their managerial tasks.

Some other important features about management development that should be noted are that:

- since development implies growth and change it is a dynamic, ongoing process;
- as a wide range of experiences and activities contribute to individual and group development it is a broader concept than training and consists of more than external courses;
- it is concerned with the development of groups of managers as well as individuals, since managers often have to work together in a team (e.g. the head and deputy headteachers);
- it aims to promote improved managerial performance – not just individual learning or career development; and
- its ultimate aim is to improve the quality of teaching and learning.

All these points are summed up in the NDC's more formal working definition, which is that 'management development is the process whereby the management function of an organisation is performed with increased effectiveness'.

More concretely, management development may be thought of as a generic term that embraces three broad components:

- *Management training* – which refers to short conferences, courses and workshops that emphasize practical information and skills, that do not normally lead to an award or qualification and that may be run by LEAs, schools or by external trainers and consultants from higher education or elsewhere.
- *Management education* – which refers mainly to secondment and fellowships and to long, external courses that often emphasize theory and research-based knowledge, and that lead to higher-education and professional qualifications (e.g. specialist school management diplomas and M Eds).
- *Management support* – which refers to those job-embedded arrangements and procedures for, for example, staff selection, promotion and career development, appraisal, job rotation, job enhancement, retirement, re-deployment and equal opportunities, and which is the responsibility of the school and the LEA.

Whom is Management Development for?

Under the terms of the DES (1987) Conditions of Employment, 'management' is now included in the professional duties of every teacher – so it can be argued that every teacher needs management development. However, at least initially, it is likely that a school's management development programme will focus on those teachers (e.g. deputy headteachers, heads of department) who have a formal managerial responsibility for one or more of the following key task areas:

- Strategic planning, including overall school policy and aims, and the school's development plan.
- Communication and decision-making structures and roles.
- Curriculum, teaching methods and examinations.
- Staff and staff development.
- Pupils and pupil learning.
- Material resources.
- External relations.
- Monitoring and evaluation of effectiveness.

These teacher–managers are also responsible for managing the process of change and development in school (e.g. when a new programme or policy, such as TVEE or local financial management, has to be introduced and established). Finally, they have some responsibility for self-development of their own professional as well as personal qualities and skills. These task areas are set out in more detail in Table 1.1.

What Activities does Management Development Involve?

The management development process encompasses a wide range of activities illustrated in Table 1.2 and many of which are described in detail in the accompanying LEA handbook. These activities can be categorized in various ways. For example, some are used to identify needs, others to promote learning and others to evaluate the learning that has taken place. Alternatively, activities can be described in terms of their degree of closeness to an individual teacher's actual job by referring to them as:

- on the job (e.g. job enhancement, appraisal, job rotation);
- close to the job (e.g. team-building, working in school with an external consultant, preparing for an interview for another post); and
- off the job (e.g. external courses and secondments).

Many teachers are promoted into posts where they have managerial responsibility on the basis of their classroom teaching experience rather than their management expertise, though headteachers and deputy heads will usually have spent some years as a middle manager (e.g. a head of department) before gaining these senior posts. Until recently there were few opportunities to receive any formal management training, and where training opportunities did exist they were frequently *ad hoc* rather than part of a systematic programme. More external management courses are now provided, although it is still the case that only a minority, albeit an increasing one, of headteachers and senior staff will have access to them. For example, NDC statistics for 1985–6 indicate that 1,719

Table 1.1   School management: main task areas

1. *Overall school policy and aims*   Philosophy, aims and objectives of the school: school development and national curriculum plans; priorities; standards; climate and ethos; equal opportunities

2. *Communication, organization and decision-making structures and roles*   Leadership and management style: working with governors, departments, faculties and other structures; methods of consultation; provision of information; communication between staff; use and resolution of conflict; staff, department and other meetings; decision-making; problem-solving; teamwork; administration (forms); staff handbook

3. *The curriculum, teaching methods and examinations*   Devising a curriculum policy in the light of the national curriuclum; curriculum implementation; development and evaluation; teaching and learning methods; subject areas; timetabling; external examinations; national testing; homework policy; cover arrangements; equal opportunities

4. *Staff and staff development*   Maintaining effective relationships with teaching and non-teaching staff of both sexes; staff appointments; incentive posts and allowances; job descriptions and specifications; pastoral care of staff; motivation; staff and management development: needs analysis, appraisal and provision of support, counselling and advice; delegation; role of staff with responsibility posts; teaching loads; probationers; student teachers; coping with stress; falling rolls; employment relations and unions; equal opportunities; INSET policy and programme related to LEA Training Grant budget and five closure days

5. *Pupils and pupil learning*   Arrangements for grouping, testing and assessment; pastoral care; record-keeping; profiles; reports; discipline; regulations; continuity of education; gender, race and special needs; social and personal development of all

6. *Finance and material resources*   Local financial management; LEA Training Grant Scheme and other budgets; buildings, equipment, furniture, materials; assessing needs; health and safety

7. *External relations*   Working with governors, LEA advisers, officers and elected members; relating to parents and wider school community; involvement of parents and governors in school; inter-school liaison; links with commerce and industry; media; support services; school and the law

8. *Monitoring and evaluation of effectiveness*   Roles and procedures (e.g. working parties); methods (e.g. GRIDS); performance indicators (e.g. exam results, intake data, etc.)

9. *Change and development*   Policy, programmes, climate, methods of review; organization development, introducing and implementing innovations (e.g. national curriculum, TVEI, local financial management)

10. *Self-development*   Self-evaluation; personal leadership style; management of time; interpersonal skills; networks; associations; courses, values

primary and secondary headteachers and senior staff took part in a 20-day or one-term management training programme, yet this was a very small proportion when one considers that there are approximately 130,000 teachers with senior management responsibilities. There is evidence that, only when participants on

Table 1.2   Examples of a range of management development activities

Off the job
- Short courses (e.g. one day)
- Long courses (e.g. 20 day)
- Award-bearing courses (e.g. M Ed)
- Fellowships (e.g. one term)
- Secondments (e.g. to industry)
- Job swap (e.g. to another school)
- Visits (e.g. to another school)
- Distance learning (e.g. Open University)
- Private study

Close to the job
- Team-building group
- School-based workshop/course
- School-based consultancy
- Selection and appointment experience
- Self-development activities
- Action-learning set

On the job
- Drawing up a job description
- Individual appraisal for development
- School self-review
- Job enhancement (e.g. acting as a project co-ordinator)
- Job rotation
- Advisory visit (e.g. from another colleague or adviser)
- Pairing with peer for mutual observation and feedback
- Planned succession experiences

such courses receive preparation and follow-up support, and when the content of the programme is negotiated between providers, LEA and the participants, do external courses become a powerful mechanism for change. A key task for schools is to explore how they can increase the longer-term benefit to the individual and the school of someone attending an external course.

A second key task for schools is to broaden their range of school-based management development activities. Research and experience both indicate that adults in professional roles learn new skills through experience, through reflecting on that experience and through receiving constructive criticism about their performance. Indeed, teachers have usually learned how to be headteachers, heads of department, etc., in practice, by doing the job on a day-to-day basis. While this experience is invaluable it could often have been enhanced if they had been helped to reflect about it more systematically and been given feedback on their performance. A school management development programme should create opportunities for effective learning to take place as close to the job as possible.

Management Development and Educational Reform

In many schools, introducing formal management development will be an innovation and teachers may be reluctant to spend time and energy on it, given the
degree of change they are already having to cope with. Yet it is the very pace and
scale of change that makes management development so important. In recent
years schools have had to deal with, for example, the introduction of TVEI,
computer studies, TRIST and LEATGS, profiling, equal opportunities and many
more innovations, at one periods and against a background of industrial action.
Recent legislation and, in particular, the Education Act 1988 has introduced a
huge additional agenda for change (e.g. appraisal, new powers for governors,
new conditions of service for teachers, local financial management, a national
curriculum and regular testing of pupils, grant maintained status). All these have
major implications for school management. The task of managing multiple, complex innovations simultaneously, whilst at the same time managing the ongoing
work of maintaining standards of teaching and learning, now dominates the
professional lives of headteachers and senior staff. They require knowledge and
skills that are not always the same as those required in classroom teaching (e.g.
interviewing, negotiating, budgeting) and heads and teachers will need management development and training as well as other forms of support if school
improvement is to be achieved. As David Styan, the leader of the School Management Task Force, put it in his 1989 interim report to the Secretary of State:

> Better schools rely ultimately on a confident and competent teaching force. Teachers
> have the right to expect well-managed schools which provide the conditions for good
> teaching and learning.
>   Heads and senior staff have the major responsibility for creating these conditions.
> They too need support, especially through this period of change and reorganisation.
> There is an urgent need for training to prepare them to manage the many elements of
> reform. Beyond this, the education service needs a sound framework for systematic
> training and development which will support heads and senior staff throughout their
> careers and prepare their successors.

What is Meant by a Management Development Policy?

If a school did have an explicit management development policy, what would it
look like? To begin with, the policy would be known within the school, it would
probably be written down and the appropriate staff would be aware what responsibility they had for management development. Arrangements would have
been made to ensure that the policy was implemented. Someone (e.g. deputy
head, professional tutor, INSET co-ordinator) would be responsible for planning, implementing and evaluating the management development policy and
programme within the broader framework of the school staff-development policy and INSET plan.

The school management development policy would balance and meet needs
arising from:

• individual teachers;

- groups or teams of teachers, for example, heads of department, a pastoral year team; and
- the whole school.

The school would have procedures for identifying individual needs (e.g. through an appraisal process), group needs (e.g. through a department review) and whole-school needs (e.g. through a school-review process).

The management development policy and programme would recognize that the individual and group needs of staff may well vary according to:

1. their age;
2. their gender and race; and
3. their job stage, in other words:

  - the preparatory stage (e.g. when they are preparing to apply for a new job);
  - the appointment stage (when they are selected or rejected);
  - the induction stage (e.g. first two years in post);
  - the in-service stage, which includes development and regeneration (e.g. 3–5, 6–10, over 11 years in post);
  - the transitional stage (e.g. promotion, re-deployment, retirement).

Equal Opportunities

Women and members of ethnic-minority groups are under-represented in managerial positions in schools in relation to their proportion in the teaching force. One long-term aim of a school management development policy could be to try to rectify this imbalance. Management development must operate and be seen to operate fairly and equitably for all teachers. This is a legal as well as a moral responsibility. Those responsible for management development should be aware of their obligations under the law on grounds of sex, race or marital status in the way in which they conduct management development, and of the danger of stereotyped expectations resulting in a biased approach. Management development should be used positively to promote equal opportunities by encouraging teachers and headteachers to fulfil their potential as school managers.

What should a School Staff try to Achieve?

Much will depend on what is already happening in school. All schools will be providing some management development and training for the staff, even though it may be on a rather *ad hoc* basis. The majority of schools probably have some form of staff-development policy and programme but many will not have made explicit provision for management development within this. Table 1.3 outlines the general characteristics of four levels of management development provision. You may find it helpful to locate your school on it and plan your strategy accordingly. So, for example, if you think that your school is at level 2 you may decide to strengthen preparation and follow-up support for teachers

Table 1.3 School management development: what level have you reached?

Level	Main observable features
1	The school • makes little management training provision of any kind for the head, senior staff and middle managers; and • makes little use of management education secondments and long courses
2	The school • has sent several teachers on external management training and education courses and secondments and has some school-based provision but this is on an *ad hoc* basis without any clear policy; • uses informal methods of identifying needs and evaluating activities; and • is only becoming aware of the 'development' approach
3	The school • has been working for several years on the evolution of a management training policy related to school improvement; • has a varied and well-established pattern of school-based activities that consist mainly of training courses; • provides some preparation and follow-up for teachers attending external courses and secondments; • has a large number of senior and junior staff who have attended external courses and secondments; • has a staff who have a reasonably common understanding of the possibilities and limitations of management training and education; and • realizes the need to adopt a development approach, including management support
4	The school • has a coherent and well-publicized policy for management development aimed at school improvement and based upon the school's development plan; • ensures that it respects equal opportunities, especially in relation to gender and race; • has procedures and staff to implement the policy in the form of a regular programme, related to the LEATGS framework; • makes use of job descriptions, appraisal interviews, school-review procedures and other methods of diagnosing needs at individual, group and whole-school level; • has a varied range of on-the-job, close-to-the-job and off-the-job activities and uses external training courses only as one component in the programme; • provides preparation and follow-up for teachers attending external courses and secondments and is able to relate such courses to individual, group and school needs; • encourages senior staff (including the headteacher) and middle managers to participate in the programme regularly; • ensures that the programme is systematically monitored and evaluated in terms of its impact on school improvement; and • ensures that the programme includes the recruitment, selection and re-deployment and retirement procedures and that both governors and the LEA are aware of this and the overall policy

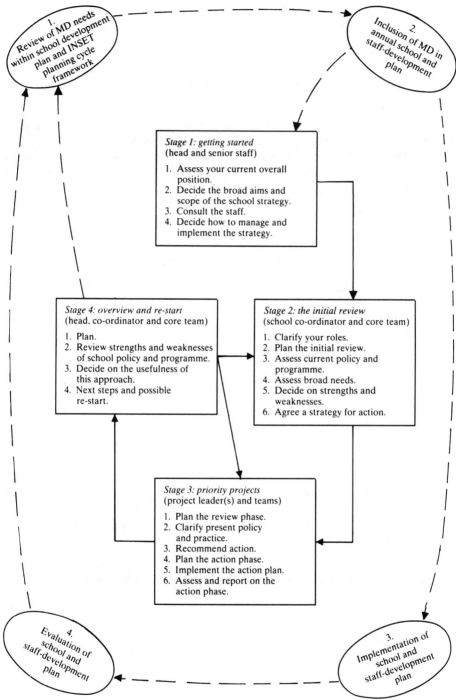

Figure 1.1 Improving Management Development in School

attending management courses. A school at level 3 may decide to broaden the range of school-based management development opportunities available to teachers or to produce an explicit policy for management development.

What is the NDC's Approach?

The NDC approach is summarized in Figure 1.1. We suggest a step-by-step approach that recognizes that a school cannot work on all aspects of its management development policy and programme simultaneously. We recommend that the head, in consultation with the staff, identifies some longer-term goals and a strategy for achieving them over an agreed period. The ongoing programme can be maintained while gradual improvements are made by working on key priority areas. The whole process can be kept under review in the context of the school staff-development policy and INSET plan.

How can this Handbook be Used?

This handbook suggests how you can formulate a policy and programme for school management development. Part II outlines the four stages of an improvement process:

Stage 1: getting started.
Stage 2: initial review.
Stage 3: priority projects.
Stage 4: overview and re-start.

Each of these stages contains a summary checklist, which is then followed by explanatory comment and illustrative examples.

In Part III we consider how you can maintain your ongoing programme of staff and management development.

A crucial decision is whether or not to try this approach at all. We suggest that you consider this question at the 'getting started' stage. If you decide to go ahead, this handbook should be seen as only one source of practical information: additional sources listed in Appendix I should be consulted as and when appropriate.

A Word about the Underlying Approach and Style

This handbook recommends a systematic approach to the improvement of the school's management development policy and programme. We recognize that such a systematic approach is often difficult, if not impossible, to adopt in complex and hectic real-life situations and, moreover, that many people prefer a less planned approach to school improvement. Headteachers and staff in this latter category adopt a more *ad hoc* approach to management development. They will probably have a rough idea of what they want to achieve; they then support any initiatives that crop up that look as if they might help them to move closer to their targets. However, because this approach is relatively unplanned it is difficult to describe, and we have found it easier to put forward our suggestions in a systematic fashion. A second point is that some of the suggestions and examples may seem obvious. Our experience is that what seems familiar and obvious in one school may be quite new to another: LEAs and schools have different policies, problems and priorities and hence are at different stages with respect to management development. Whenever possible we have included examples to illustrate the points we are making.

PART II
IMPROVING MANAGEMENT
DEVELOPMENT IN SCHOOL

There are five chapters in this part, one on each stage of the improvement process and one containing two case studies of school management development in practice. In a large school it is likely that several teachers will be working on management development and they may be involved at different stages in the process. Potentially there is a rather different audience for each chapter though in practice some staff (e.g. a deputy headteacher) will probably be involved throughout. The five chapters are as follows:

Chapter 2   Stage 1: getting started   Addressed to the headteacher and senior management team.

Chapter 3   Stage 2: initial review   Addressed to the school management development co-ordinator and the core team.

Chapter 4   Stage 3: priority projects   Addressed to the project leader and team and the school management development co-ordinator.

Chapter 5   Stage 4: overview and re-start   Addressed to the school management development co-ordinator, the core team and the headteacher.

Chapter 6   Two case studies   Addressed to everyone who has some involvement with the management development policy and programme.

UWCC LIBRARY

2

GETTING STARTED ON SYSTEMATIC MANAGEMENT DEVELOPMENT

This chapter is addressed mainly to the headteacher and the members of the senior management team. Experience clearly indicates that the headteacher's active support is essential if major innovations are to take root and flourish in a school. Management development goes right to the heart of the school's organization and so it has implications for the headteacher as much as, if not more than, for other members of staff.

A focus on management development will inevitably have implications for resources, and it is useful to reflect at the outset on the advantages and disadvantages of moving to a more systematic approach. Initially, the headteacher may want to consider these questions alone, although it is usually advisable to discuss the matter with some colleagues (e.g. the deputy headteachers) from the outset.

Your initial decision may be just an agreement in principle to consider more carefully what the school's position on management development and training is. Once this has been agreed it should not take too long to decide whether or not to move to a more systematic approach. The four main steps suggested here are summarized in Checklist 2.1 and described below. The steps are intended to be carried out quickly. Experience indicates that the whole of stage 1 can be completed during a couple of meetings (e.g. not stretching over more than half a term and possibly much shorter).

Step 1: Assess the School's Current Overall Position on Management Development

You can do this by referring to Table 1.3 on p. 10 and Checklists 2.2 and 2.3. The different levels of management development activity outlined in Table 1.3 are broad generalizations and will not fit any school exactly. Nevertheless, the table may act as a stimulus to thought and discussion if you try to locate your school on

Checklist 2.1 Stage 1: getting started on systematic management development – key steps for the headteacher and senior management team

---

Step 1

Assess your current overall position.

Tasks

1. Estimate what the level of management development provision is in your school (see Table 1.3, p. 10).
2. Identify the main relevant features of your school's structure and organization.
3. Consider what priority is given to management development in your overall policy and funding for staff development.

Step 2

Decide the broad aims and scope of the school management development strategy.

Tasks

1. Agree what level you want to aim for in the medium and long terms and how you might achieve this (Table 1.3, p. 10).
2. Consider the implications of using the NDC approach to management development and decide whether it would be appropriate in your school.

Step 3

Consult the staff.

Tasks

1. Explain to the appropriate staff why you wish to work on management development.
2. Describe the NDC approach to management development and consider any alternatives.
3. Assess staff reaction.
4. Decide whether or not to:

   (a) work on management development;
   (b) follow the NDC approach.

Step 4

Decide how to manage and implement the strategy.

Tasks

1. Decide:

   (a) who should be designated as co-ordinator; and
   (b) whether you want to establish a core team.

2. Agree on their terms of reference, including broad goals and timetable.
3. Agree on a procedure for informing and consulting colleagues.
4. Consider whom else (e.g. LEA adviser) might be consulted or involved and how best to do this.

it. You may realize, for instance, that provision is uneven and that while you and the deputies have received a considerable amount of development and training, few other teachers have received any.

The NDC approach is intended to help you move towards a more systematic approach to management development in school and to improve and strengthen existing practice. Many schools will already be doing a great deal though it may not be formally identified as management development. These quotations from two headteachers illustrate this point:

> There is an overall and tacitly acknowledged aim of developing staff to reach their full potential, both in the furtherance of their own careers and in their usefulness to the school, but this has developed in a fairly pragmatic, haphazard way on an individual basis. There is neither history nor experience of a systematic coherent form of staff or management development.

> The staff development policy is implicit within a number of the activities which take place rather than through a published programme. We have used the normal management structure and the various reviews of school activities to develop staff professionally by their participation, e.g. job descriptions, job rotations, encouragement of staff to attend specific courses to help them, etc.

The questions in Checklist 2.2a and b should also help you to review the level you have reached. If you find that most or all of the features mentioned on the checklist have been in place for some time and that a reasonably high proportion of the senior staff and middle managers have already received some form of management training, then you are probably already at level 2 or 3 and can set your long-term targets accordingly. Alternatively, if there are many aspects that have not yet been considered and few teachers have received any management training, then you might need to consider how you can increase the number of people who have some knowledge and understanding of management development (e.g. by sending one or two people on an external management course).

The question in Checklist 2.3 should help you to reflect systematically about the character of the school. Your answers should help you to decide how and when to move forward on management development. For example, if you have no professional tutor or INSET organizer, who would co-ordinate any work on management development? If the procedures for consulting staff about policy

Checklist 2.2a   Management development – what is the position in your school?

	In place for some time	Just started	Planned but not yet in place	Not yet considered
Task allocations				
Managerial responsibilities are clearly allocated to particular staff				
School-specific job descriptions exist for:				
• the head				
• the deputies				
• senior teachers				
• heads of department/year				
• all teachers				
There is a staff handbook that explains how the school is organized and managed				
This handbook contains staff job descriptions and is regularly updated				
Needs identification				
There is a system of individual teacher appraisal for:				
• the head				
• the deputies				
• senior teachers				
• heads of department/year				
• all teachers				
There is a system of self-review/evaluation for:				
• departments/year/pastoral teams				
• the school as a whole				
There are established procedures for consulting staff				

	In place for some time	Just started	Planned but not yet in place	Not yet considered
Policy There is a written policy statement on: • the organization and the curriculum • staff and management development and training • equal opportunities *Meeting identified needs* A senior member of staff is responsible for staff development (e.g. professional tutor) There is an annual progamme of staff and management development activities that: • includes a variety of school-based activities as well as external courses • includes provision for giving briefing and follow-up support to staff who attend external courses • is monitored and evaluated, e.g. system for evaluating external and school-based INSET; evaluation tasks allocated in job descriptions				

If many of these features have been in place for some time or have been recently introduced, it is likely that your school is ready to establish a systematic management development programme. Alternatively, if few of these things have yet been considered you may need to begin by clarifying the structure.

matters are somewhat inadequate, how would you institute a debate about management development?

Consider finally what proportion of effort and resources have been devoted to management development within the overall staff-development programme. Where schools have their own INSET budget it may be possible to answer this question very precisely. In most cases you will only be able to make a rough estimate: how many of the external courses attended by staff and the

Checklist 2.2b   Experience of management development and training

Attended some time in last three years	Support and training	Training			Education	
	School-based management development and training activities	LEA short management course (e.g. 2–3 days)	Other short INSET management course	Long INSET course, e.g. 20-day management	One-term course/ fellowship	Award-bearing course (e.g. M Ed and OU degree or diploma)
Head						
Deputy 1						
Deputy 2						
Senior teachers						
Heads of department:						
• a few						
• less than 50%						
• more than 50%						
• all						
Pastoral heads:						
• a few						
• less than 50%						
• more than 50%						
• all						
Other staff:						
• a few						
• less than 50%						
• more than 50%						
• all						

How aware are your staff of management development? If most of the people listed above have received some form of management training in the last three years, then it is likely that at minimum you have a common language and concepts and are ready to move forward. If few, or none, have received any management development and training, then you may need to try to raise awareness (e.g. by sending one or two people on a management course) before trying to establish a systematic management development programme.

Checklist 2.3   Basic questions about school management development

1. What priority in terms of time and money is given to management development within the wider staff-development programme and INSET budget?
2. How are management development needs identified?

   - Individual (e.g. appraisal)?
   - School (e.g. school self-review)?
   - For groups of staff (e.g. questionnaire to heads of department)?
   - In relation to career stage (e.g. periodic interviews)?
   - In relation to equal opportunities (e.g. specific questionnaire for women teachers)?

3. How is the use of external management courses planned?

   - By the head?
   - By the professional tutor/INSET co-ordinator?
   - By staff-development committee?
   - By individuals?

4. How are school-based management development activities planned?

   - By the headteacher?
   - By the professional tutor?
   - By a staff-development committee?

5. How are staff consulted?

   - By whole staff meetings?
   - By group meetings (e.g. senior management team, faculty heads)?
   - By questionnaire?
   - By letter (e.g. being asked to comment on policy documents)?

6. How are management development activities

   - supported (e.g. preparation and follow-up);
   - monitored; and
   - evaluated?

7. Is the selection and appointment process seen as part of the management development process?

school-based activities were concerned with management? Is there an induction programme for new heads of department as well as for probationers? If very little has been done in the past you may need to begin with some awareness-raising to help staff realize that management development should be a priority.

Step 2: Decide the Broad Aims and Scope of the School Strategy

Look again at Table 1.3 (p. 10). Once you have made a rough assessment of the school's current position on management development, consider what level you aim to reach in the medium term (e.g. two years) and longer term (e.g. five years). The NDC approach is aimed at level 4 and is intended to help you to develop a systematic approach to management development and training. However, adopting this approach will have practical consequences. For example, it is suggested that someone is nominated as management development co-ordinator and is given some time to do the job.

Obviously, you will need to take account of what is feasible and appropriate as well as desirable. There is a limit to the number of innovations any school can handle. If one of the deputy headteachers is on secondment, if you are training staff to implement appraisal, financial management and the new curriculum and if an HMI inspection is planned, it is probably not a good moment to start on systematic management development! On the other hand, there will never be a perfect time to begin, and management development should, in the long term, help the staff to cope better with multiple innovations.

This comment from the head of a special school helps to illustrate this point:

> Four years ago when I was appointed as a head, I formulated plans for the school which I discussed with my new deputy on his appointment. We agreed upon priority areas of school organisation and curriculum and have gradually worked through these, appointing new staff to help initiate the changes. New areas for progress are ear-marked each year, priorities being noted. These decisions have then been discussed with senior staff and in some cases with the staff as a whole, but we have now realised that it is impossible to make long term plans because we are aware that in the next 2/3 years there may be far reaching changes in the structure of and criteria for admission to our school. This has implications for the development of staff and curriculum and requires a wider perspective on training and deployment of staff and resources.

One response, when faced with a situation like this, might be for the head and senior management team to postpone additional work on management development until the dust settles and tasks and roles can be more clearly defined. Alternatively, they could decide to strengthen their management development programme with the expectation that this will help the staff to become better managers and so enable the school to cope more easily with change.

The scale of the exercise also needs thought. Would it be more sensible to begin by working on the management development needs of the head and deputy headteachers or should all the teachers with a formal managerial responsibility be included? In special schools should all the professional staff be included or just the teachers? If women are under-represented in senior posts, should there be some specific management development activities for women teachers? Look through the rest of this handbook, consider the implications of the NDC approach and decide whether or not it would be appropriate in your school at the moment.

Of course, we recognize that it is not easy to decide on an appropriate approach. The question raised by this headteacher may be echoed by others:

How can we best pierce the defences of fairly senior, long serving staff who feel threatened when their effectiveness is questioned and ways sought to improve their performance? At this school there is likely to be considerable scepticism from a substantial number of Heads of Department who have been in post for more than the past decade.

The most obvious piece of advice is that you should be sensitive to individual concerns and if possible ask people to express them and to try to deal with them at the outset.

Another head decided on a pragmatic approach: 'I decided that as over thirty members of the staff had managerial responsibilities and could benefit from a management development programme, that a programme for all thirty should be spread over three years with approximately 10–12 in a group for each year'.

The questions in Checklist 2.4 should help you reflect how you wish to proceed.

Checklist 2.4   How do you intend to proceed?

---

1. What priority will management development have in the school's overall staff-development plan (and budget if there is one)?
2. Do you intend to start with all the 'managers' in school or only a few of them (e.g. the deputy headteachers)?
3. Do you intend to look at all areas of management or focus on a particular managerial task (e.g. one that seems in urgent need of improvement)?
4. What do you intend to start on?

   • Clarifying roles and tasks by writing/reviewing job descriptions?
   • Strengthening the needs identification process?
   • Strengthening preparation and follow-up for external courses?
   • Strengthening school-based management development activities?
   • Other?

5. What approach is feasible given the climate and culture of your school? For example, if an 'organic' or *ad hoc* approach to change is the norm, what would be necessary to introduce a rational planning or systematic approach such as the one described in this handbook?

Step 3: Consult the Staff

Since management development may be a major innovation that could have a big impact on the school, it is important that you consult those teachers who are likely to be affected by the strategy from the outset. It is crucial to try to establish a favourable climate for management development. One way of doing this is to make it clear that the head is included as well as other teachers, and to try to demonstrate by example that, as members of the senior management team, you are personally committed to management development. Another strategy is to talk through what management development means with the teachers who are likely to be involved and attempt to deal with any concerns they might have. You will almost certainly want to discuss the matter with the middle managers (e.g. heads of department, heads of year) either individually or as a group. If you decide to discuss the matter with staff on an individual basis, confusion and anxiety will be reduced if you can see everyone in a relatively short space of time. At some point you may want to raise the matter with the whole staff.

One issue you may have to face is that many teachers do not really see themselves as managers. The majority of teachers spend the bulk of their time working in classrooms with children; for many this is the main source of their professional identity and satisfaction. Though they might agree with the broader definition that says they have some responsibility for the work of other adults (e.g. as a head of department for the other teachers in the department), this can fit uneasily with a view of the professional autonomy of the teacher. This comment by the head of a special school could probably be echoed by many other headteachers:

> I would query whether 'manager' is the correct word to use. Whilst it may be related to the development of management skills in teachers in schools for the benefit of pupils, teachers do not see themselves as 'managers'. Management is still a top level function and teachers only perceive the head as the manager. A business has only one 'manager' and they consider that the headteacher should be able to fulfil this role in the same way as, for example, the manager of the local bank.

She went on to argue that

> Teachers need to see that the head is capable of managing and that some professional training is needed to prepare the head for this onerous task. Teachers themselves need to learn how to organise and manage and can be prepared by their head for different levels of responsibility. . . . Although staff want to feel involved in the development of the school, a too democratic approach can undermine their confidence in the head-teacher. They prefer to feel that the head is able to make decisions and is in control of all situations, not someone who is only nominally a head.

Even when teachers do see themselves as managers, they have little time available for this aspect of their role. Given that the main responsibility of the majority of staff is classroom teaching, managerial tasks have to be fitted into the spaces that remain in the day. School management can be a hidden activity. Consultation may need to begin with some awareness-raising work about the managerial tasks that have to be dealt with in school (Table 1.1 (p. 6) could be used as a stimulus to discussion). Alternatively you might ask a group of teachers (e.g. heads of house/year and their teams) to list all the things they do as part of their job in addition to classroom teaching. Then discuss these and identify the ones that could properly be described as management tasks.

This comment by a secondary head indicated that he hoped to raise staff-awareness of management tasks if he did nothing else:

> The responses from the teachers did indicate the enormous expectations that are placed on senior staff. They are expected to be professional leaders, in the classroom exhibiting good practice, trouble shooters coming like knights in armour to the aid of teachers in distress, always available to deal with problems of professional development or school management. It is somewhat ironic that few actually recognised that senior staff had tasks in their own right, presumably to be performed in twilight time. An important part of management development must be to heighten awareness of the managerial role that all staff, and in particular senior staff, have.

In practice, as might be expected, headteachers have very different views about and styles of consultation with staff. These examples illustrate three different approaches:

> I am a traditional, autocratic paternalist – but, I hope, an entirely benign one. I decided to work on management development and told the senior staff – I believe in consultation as a matter of courtesy, but I reserve the right to make the decisions.

> Consultation with vice principals only at first. The decision was taken with them and the staff were informed later.

> We are working on management development because the staff were consulted and agreed. . . . A note was placed in the staff section of the News Sheet and a notice placed on the staff room notice board. 37 staff attended the voluntary meeting. . . . Having consulted those who were interested, and they included almost all staff mostly involved with the school management structure, and discussed their response in detail within an inner cabinet of head and deputy heads, it was decided to proceed and inform all staff.

You will need to assess staff reaction and weigh this in the balance when deciding whether or not to proceed with management development. Some of the varied reasons headteachers gave for deciding to work on management development are listed below:

> To achieve a better understanding of management roles in school and thereby improve our own performance.

> A recent HMI report prodded us in the direction of developing managing skills.

> We expect that we shall achieve better educational results as a consequence of improving staff management performance at all levels. In particular, we hope to improve our skills in the management of time and improve our communications.

> Other factors which influenced the decision were: that I was the one most threatened and was happy to go ahead; management development is coming in education and it was better for us to influence it than non-teachers or industrial executives; if there are identifiable and trainable management skills it would be to our individual and collective benefit.

If the staff are keen to strengthen and to increase the provision of management development in school, discuss with them possible ways of moving forward.

Outline the NDC approach and check if they would like to follow this or if they would prefer to adopt some alternative strategy.

Step 4: Decide how to Manage and Implement the Strategy

If you decide to follow this approach to systematic management development, then a key recommendation is that someone is given the task of co-ordinating the whole strategy. In many ways the person who is best place to do this is the headteacher. The dilemma, however, is that he or she may not be able to allocate time on a regular basis to do the job. Given that headteachers invariably have a 'vision' of the type of school they are trying to establish and that this influences the way the school is organized and managed, then they must be centrally involved with any management development policy and programme. But if they cannot allocate time to co-ordinate the work on a day-to-day basis this task is best delegated to someone else (e.g. a deputy headteacher). If one of the deputy headteachers has a specific responsibility for staff development then this would be the ideal person. The systematic style of working suggested in this handbook will probably require an investment of at least two to three hours a week by the co-ordinator. If at all possible it is preferable to set aside a regular period each week for this task so as to try to avoid the danger that other things squeeze it out.

You may also want to consider identifying a small group to advise on the management development policy. This could be especially useful at the outset when you are working out your ideas. It could consist of just three or four members of staff but it may be helpful to include one or two other people, for example, your school's pastoral adviser, a governor, someone (a parent?) with management training experience. The advantages of such a group are that it provides a forum for discussing policy issues, and knowledge and understanding of the management development process is shared. If you set up some form of core group or team do try to locate them within the existing decision-making structure (e.g. if you have a staff-development committee, they could become a subgroup of this). If you want the management development group to have some influence over existing practice and emerging policy then they must have access to the appropriate communication and decision-making structure in the school.

The co-ordinator and core team (if there is one) will need clear terms of reference, in other words, the scope of the task, what outcomes are expected and what resources are available. If the co-ordinator is not the head then some arrangement will be needed for reviewing the strategy with the head. It is sensible to formalize this by, for example, agreeing that the headteacher and the co-ordinator should meet to discuss management development every Wednesday from 3.30 to 4.00 p.m., rather than leave such meetings to occur by chance. It will obviously be beneficial if such meetings can be fitted into directed time. Consider also how to keep other members of staff informed about what is happening. The staff most directly involved are probably the priority here but it might be beneficial to keep everyone informed and to raise awareness of school management.

Needless to say, your plans will have to be considered in the context of the teachers' Conditions of Employment. Is work on management development to be a voluntary activity for the teachers involved? How much can be done within directed time – for example, within the regular cycle of meetings? Would it be feasible to allocate one of the staff in-service days to this work?

Finally, consider whom else should or could be consulted or involved in work on management development and think how best to do this. Obvious candidates are the members of the school governing body and someone from the team of LEA advisers and officers. However, there may well be others, for example, a headteacher in a neighbouring school or a local industrialist whom it would be useful to contact.

3
THE INITIAL REVIEW

In this chapter we assume that the headteacher and staff have decided to follow the NDC approach and start some work on management development. We make the further assumption that someone, who is probably not the head but may be a deputy headteacher, has been designated as school management development co-ordinator. A small core team of teachers may have also volunteered or been asked to work on the management development policy and programme. So the people addressed as 'you' in this chapter are the school management development co-ordinator and the members of the core team.

The suggestions made here are intended to help you review your existing practice in management development and to decide upon an appropriate strategy for moving forward (see Checklist 3.1). In particular, they should assist you to identify priority topics to work on in the year ahead. We recognize that, with the head, you will have to continue to manage the school and will have to maintain the ongoing staff and management development programme while this is happening. It is also quite possible that, if the school is just beginning to do some work on management development, much of the information you might like to draw upon will not be easily available (e.g. no system for school review in place; no records of in-service activities attended). Our advice is to do what you can with the information available. The initial review should be as systematic and thorough as possible, but it should not be so lengthy that it leads to paralysis. The central purpose is to identify priorities before planning a programme of management development activities.

The key tasks that need to be considered at the initial-review stage are discussed below. The timing will vary depending on how you decide to address them but, whichever approach you adopt, this stage should probably not last more than a term.

Checklist 3.1   Stage 2: the initial review – key steps for the co-ordinator and core team

---

Step 1

Clarify your role as co-ordinator.

Tasks

1. Check your terms of reference and the extent of your authority, and agree procedures for keeping colleagues informed about what you do.
2. Clarify the working relationship between yourself and the core team.
3. Check that you have been allocated sufficient resources to do the job.

Step 2

Plan the initial review.

Tasks

1. Agree a short but realistic timetable for the initial review.
2. Decide if you need any help from outsiders (e.g. LEA advisers, school governors) at this stage and if so make the necessary arrangements.
3. Agree on a procedure for writing a report on the initial review.

Step 3

Clarify the nature and extent of the school's present policy and programme for management development.

Tasks

1. Review any relevant school-policy papers.
2. Identify any school-based management training activities.
3. Check what external management training opportunities are available for staff and how many of the staff have been on an external management training course in the last three years.
4. Check what procedures are used in school for:

- staff selection and appointment;
- drawing up and updating job descriptions; and
- identifying needs.

Step 4

Make a preliminary assessment of broad needs.

Tasks

1. Identify any management development needs arising from LEA or national policy initiatives.
2. Check what management development needs have been highlighted in:

   - the school development plan;
   - group/departmental reviews; and
   - individual teacher reviews/appraisals.

3. Identify priority areas for management development in one or more of the following ways:

   - Using a questionnaire.
   - Using a structured group discussion.
   - Informal interviews with teachers/appraisal.
   - Doing it yourself.

Step 5

Decide on strengths and weaknesses.

Tasks

1. Synthesize the conclusions from steps 3 and 4.
2. Identify those features of the current policy and ongoing programme that are satisfactory and should be maintained.
3. Identify any unsatisfactory features of the existing programme and areas where it is not meeting needs. Distinguish between those needs that:

   (a) should be dealt with as specific priority projects in the short or medium term; and
   (b) are better dealt with in the long term.

Step 6

Agree a step-by-step strategy for achieving systematic management development.

Tasks

1. Agree the aims and scope of the strategy and a realistic timetable (e.g. one, three or five years), including a provisional date for the periodic review.
2. Identify available resources.
3. Identify likely barriers and ways of overcoming them.
4. Draw up some recommendations for action and consult colleagues about them.
5. Decide on next steps for the year ahead.

Step 1: Clarify your Role as Co-ordinator

We have said that the co-ordinator may or may not be the headteacher. Where a deputy headteacher or someone else has taken on this role, an important first task is to clarify the terms of reference and the limits of authority. What are you expected to undertake and produce? It is essential that the headteacher is kept closely informed about what is happening, so procedures for doing this and for informing colleagues will need to be agreed. If a core team has been set up you will need to decide how you are going to work together. Will you meet on a regular basis? How much time can the teachers concerned allocate to this work? How formal should the meetings be? Are there any potential problems arising from status imbalances that should be dealt with? Each school will have a different answer to these questions, but given that time will inevitably be in short supply, it is important that meetings are used profitably, for example, that there are agendas, that notes are made of decisions taken and deadlines agreed. In the schools involved in the NDC's original management development project, the headteacher was nominated as co-ordinator and designated another person, usually a deputy but in one instance a senior head of year, as deputy or assistant co-ordinator. One school set up a formal management development advisory committee:

> 15 staff volunteered and others said they were prepared to serve on working parties. Composition of the committee was discussed within the inner cabinet following individual submissions from them. . . . They were prepared to accept that the deputy coordinator and I would keep them informed of all developments. This enabled more staff at different management levels to become involved including a newly appointed, main professional grade colleague. The final committee of 8 staff was unanimously agreed by the inner cabinet.

Even if you decide not to set up a formal committee, talk through your ideas on management development with colleagues in order to generate new ideas and suggestions and to help colleagues develop a sense of ownership of the emerging management development policy.

You should also try to ensure that you have the necessary resources to do the job. Time is likely to be the most crucial factor. We estimated at the outset that the co-ordinator will need on average two to three hours a week. If at all possible it is useful to build in periods of 'protected' time free from interruptions, though this will not be easy. Similarly, any meetings with teachers about management development should, where possible, be included in directed time in the school day and not always regarded as an additional voluntary commitment at the end of the afternoon. This comment from the head of a special school illustrates the difficulties:

> My problem is mainly one of implementation because of the pressures of day to day school life: pupils, staff and parents with either 'problems' or matters clearly deserving immediate attention, minor crises, etc. which take up vast amounts of the head's time and the time of the senior team in an EPA school.

Step 2: Plan the Initial Review

The initial review is intended to be systematic and thorough but not especially lengthy. We recommend that you do not spend more than a term on it. However, you must decide when it would be appropriate to make a start. Inevitably there will be some resource implications – for example, you may well identify management training needs in areas you consider a priority. It is sensible to anticipate this and try to build some resources for management development into your budget from the outset. The new procedure for funding in-service (LEATGS) usually involves schools identifying their in-service needs in the summer term so that the LEA can submit a bid for INSET funds to the Department of Education and Science in the following September. Some schools now have their own in-service budget or are a member of a consortium of schools with access to a joint INSET budget. Ideally the work on management development should fit in with the cycle of decision-making on in-service. If you make a bid for funding for management development activities in September, by the following April (when you will probably be moving into the action stage), some resources should be available.

Consider whether it would be useful to have any help from people outside the staff at this stage. Much will depend on who is available and how staff are likely to react. Opinion on when to involve non-teachers varies. Several schools sought the active participation of members of the governing body from the outset:

> At an early stage I brought the governors into discussions and there is now a regular item on management development in my governors' report.

> The vice chairman of governors had considerable managerial experience, was director of a subsidiary of a major national company and had been the PTA treasurer; following governors' discussions he was prepared to join the school's management development steering/advisory committee.

Others, however, felt that initially only the staff should be involved: 'the school is still analysing the results of the first questionnaires [used to identify management development needs] and until this is complete there would be no role for an outsider to play'.

Some staff would welcome help with the whole process whereas others are content to identify their priorities and then invite in people who have expertise in these specific areas. However, when there is someone available who has relevant experience it would seem a pity not to use it.

The initial review may be conducted by the whole staff or a small group of teachers. If the whole staff are to be consulted fully about the management development policy and programme, then every teacher (and anyone else involved) needs to have access to some form of report on the outcomes of the review – preferably a written one. As part of your preliminary planning, consider what type of report you want to produce and who should be responsible for this.

Step 3: Clarify the Nature and Extent of the School's Present Policy and Programme for Management Development

There is probably a great deal going on in school but it is unlikely to be formally labelled management development. A starting-point is to review any relevant existing documents, for example, the staff handbook, the staff-development policy, job descriptions, etc. This should help to clarify current policy. For example, one school reported that the 'deputies and the head have specific departmental attachments which include the task of fostering the professional development of colleagues'. The school staff-development programme may specify particular development opportunities.

Next, try to identify what actually happens in practice. Much of this may be informal:

> School based management training activities are mainly in the 'self-help' area. For example I was a Director of Studies and a timetabler in the 1970's and will involve all interested members of the senior team and heads of department in timetabling tutorials as I work on the timetable this term.

Many other management development activities and opportunities may be available. Examples include:

- deputy headteachers exchanging areas of responsibility;
- junior members of staff being asked to chair meetings, write reports and papers, etc.;
- school-based in-service sessions on chairing meetings, report-writing, etc;
- shadowing a colleague at work (e.g. a more junior colleague observing a head of year);
- a wide range of staff being given experience of selection and interviewing;
- individual career-counselling and help in writing a curriculum vitae; and
- a deputy 'standing in' for the headteacher.

You may have already identified several of these if you completed Checklist 2.2 (pp. 20–2). Learning by doing, ideally through practice in the job and reflection on this practice, is likely to be fruitful. In giving an individual a different and challenging task to tackle you are providing an opportunity for development; however, if you also provide some advance preparation and feedback once the task has been completed, then it is much more likely that the individual will be able to develop and change. This comment by a special-school headteacher serves as a reminder that though teachers are given managerial tasks these are frequently not regarded as training opportunities:

> The work done in the school for staff development has never previously been consciously regarded as management training. Members of staff have discharged their responsibilities of planning and organisation following mutual consultation and according to the needs of the school. I feel the present staff cope well with managerial problems which arise in the course of their work, with experience and commonsense being the major supports.

The learning process might be speeded up if some of this experience and common sense could be shared from the outset. Management development needs can arise in relation to tasks that may be inherently difficult (e.g. negotiating with professional-association representatives during a period of industrial action) or that are new for the individual or group concerned (e.g. handling the devolved school budget).

Identifying school-based management development activities that meet these needs will not be an easy task if they are all informal. One strategy might be to organize a meeting for the key 'managers' in school (e.g. head, deputy head-teachers, heads of department) and ask them to brainstorm a list of management development opportunities they have access to and ones they make available to the staff for whom they are responsible.

Identifying external management development opportunities should be an easier task. Check how many of the staff have been on a management training course recently (see Checklist 2.2b, p. 22). The LEA in-service booklet should indicate the scope of the LEA management training and education programme.

Step 4: Make a Preliminary Assessment of Broad Needs

The first task here should not be too difficult. Reflect on existing school policy and innovations and any LEA or national policy initiatives the school is involved with and consider what management training needs they throw up. For example, if the school has been asked to produce a system of local financial management, at least one member of staff will have to learn far more about financial management.

Major innovations, such as TVEE or pupil profiling, usually require that someone is designated as school co-ordinator. These school co-ordinators may have to chair staff meetings, advise and support colleagues, write materials, liaise with external agencies, etc. They will usually be working in interdisciplinary teams, cutting across departments. All these tasks may well generate management training needs as may the statementing procedure for children in special schools. Individual management development needs can also arise from someone's role or job stage (e.g. a newly appointed head of department, a head of year who wishes to apply for a deputy headship, an experienced woman main professional-grade teacher who wants more managerial experience). One or two people can probably note down fairly quickly all the potential management training needs arising from school, LEA and national policies.

The second task – clarifying what management development needs have been highlighted in the school development plan and through individual teacher and departmental/group reviews – may prove more difficult. In an ideal world each school would have in place systematic processes for reviewing the school (e.g. ILEA, *Keeping the School under Review*, 1988), for identifying group needs and for identifying individual needs (e.g. teacher appraisal). Management development needs would be identified with other staff-development needs through these regular procedures. However, many schools have not yet achieved this. There is no reason to delay making a start on systematic management development until you have systems for school review and appraisal in place. Indeed, a medium-term objective for your management development strategy might be to introduce more formal procedures for identifying needs if you decided this was a priority.

How might you identify management development needs in the interim? Four possible approaches you might want to consider are suggested here:

Option 1: questionnaire survey of staff opinion.
Option 2: structured group discussion.
Option 3: interviews with individual members of staff.
Option 4: headteacher selects priority area(s).

You must decide which approach would be most appropriate. The factors most likely to influence your choice are:

- your personal management style;
- the intended scope of the exercise (i.e. senior management and team only, heads of department, or the whole staff); and
- whether you want to start by focusing on broad managerial tasks (school needs) or on individual management development needs.

Option 1: Questionnaire Survey of Staff Opinion

The questionnaire in Example 3.1 focuses on broad managerial tasks for the whole staff. If you already have a system for school self-review in place, you would probably not need to conduct this survey since the school review should identify priority task areas. The questionnaire given as an example here should help you to highlight particular task areas in school where the management might be tightened up. For example, there may be nothing wrong in principle with the procedures for communication in school, difficulties may arise from the way in which they are interpreted and used.

Example 3.1   Survey of staff opinion about managerial task areas that could usefully be worked on this year

In column 1 – Please tick up to two managerial task areas you think it would be useful to work on this year.

In column 2 – Please tick up to two managerial task areas you think it would be useful to work on in the medium term, for example, over the next two years.

In column 3 – Please indicate which aspect(s) you want to focus on and give reasons for your choice.

	1	2	3
	It would be useful to work on this area:		Aspects of the task that should be focused on and my reasons for this choice
	immediately (e.g. this year)	in the medium term (e.g. next year)	
Managing the overall school policy			
Managing the school communication and decision-making structures and roles			
Managing the curriculum, teaching methods and examinations			
Managing staff and staff development			
Managing pupils and pupil learning			
Managing financial and material resources			
Managing external relations			
Managing the process of monitoring and evaluating the work of the school			
Managing change and development			
Managing personal self-development			

Read through the questionnaire and the accompanying notes before deciding whether or not it would be appropriate for you to use it. If you decide that you would like a large group, possibly all of the staff, to complete the survey sheet, you will need to ensure that you have some help to administer it and to collate the results.

Administering the questionnaire

Since by this stage you and the headteacher will have talked to some or all of the staff about management development, some shared understanding of what it means should be emerging. Nevertheless, before issuing the questionnaire, it is advisable to arrange a short meeting for all the staff who are going to be invited to complete it. Use this meeting to clarify:

- the purpose of the questionnaire survey;
- how you intend to administer it;
- what the managerial tasks in school are (see Table 1.1, p. 6); and
- what you understand by management development (see p. 7).

Finally, hand out the questionnaire and agree a time when it should be returned. (Do not allow too long a gap – two or three days at most.) The questionnaire should not take more than 30 minutes to complete but you may find that colleagues prefer to take it home to return next day.

Fix a date for a further meeting when the survey results will be discussed.

Remember our suggestion that the whole of this initial-review stage should not last more than a term. If you decide to use the questionnaire you should try to see that it does not take more than half a term to complete and analyse.

Collating the questionnaire responses

A suggested procedure here is, first, to tally the responses in section 1 by making a simple frequency count, for example:

Managerial task area	*No. of people who said it would be useful to work on this area*
Managing the overall policy	4
Managing the school communication and decision-making structures	12

For section 2 write down all the comments under the different heads (Table 3.1).

Consider how you are going to present the survey findings. If only a small number of teachers have filled in the questionnaire you may be able to reproduce all the written responses. However, if large numbers of people are involved you will probably have to synthesize the comments.

If possible, give everyone concerned a copy of the results before the meeting – an informed discussion is only really possible when everyone has access to the information. If for some reason you are unable to do this, at least put the results

Table 3.1   Collating the questionnaire responses

Managerial task area	No. of mentions	Aspect	Reasons
Managing the overall policy	1		
Managing the school communication and decision-making structures			
Managing staff	2	Individual development	We need an opportunity to talk through our career development with someone
		Role of the head of department	I am unsure how much authority I have over teachers in my department

on a large sheet (possibly displayed on a noticeboard?) or on an overhead-projector transparency and use this at the meeting.

Interpreting the survey results

Once the survey data have been collated it is advisable to meet with colleagues (i.e. the people who completed the survey) to discuss the results. This meeting will have two broad purposes:

- To discuss the results and to clarify what the responses mean exactly (some of the written comments will probably be ambiguous).
- To decide what, in the opinion of the school staff, are the managerial task areas that should be a priority for work in the year ahead, and which areas are a longer-term priority.

Ideally, the head should chair the meeting. A suggested procedure is to take people through the results to try to clarify any ambiguities. Try to seek consensus about what the immediate priority areas are, but if this is not easy organize a vote.

The outcome of this discussion will determine some but not all the priority areas for the management development programme in the year ahead, since some balance will have to be drawn between these and individual management development needs.

Other approaches

There are, of course, many alternative questionnaires you may prefer to use including, for example, the one developed by Cyril Poster and Michael Murphy (1987 – see Appendix I).

Option 2: Structured Group Discussion

This is an alternative way of getting the staff's view about what the priority management task areas for the school are. It contrasts with option 1 (the questionnaire) in that teachers are encouraged to write down management development needs as they see them, whereas in the questionnaire they are asked to consider needs under ten broad headings.

This method of group discussion:

- should promote a wider understanding of management development among the teachers and help to build up their commitment to it;
- should help to bring about more collaborative work in school;
- can improve the head's as well as teachers' skills in sharing decision-making; and
- should enable all the teachers involved to express an opinion, not just those who are vocal in discussion groups.

The procedure consists of:

1. an initial planning meeting;
2. a discussion with the staff concerned; and
3. a second discussion with the same group of staff a few days later.

Initial planning meeting

Discuss the structured group discussion method first with a senior colleague and enlist their support – you will need someone to help you to collate information after the initial meeting and to record decisions at later meetings. Decide how many of the staff should be involved: senior management team only? Senior management team plus middle managers (heads of department and heads of year)? It would not be particularly easy to run a discussion of this type with the full staff if this meant 60 or 70 teachers – 20 to 30 people would be easier to handle.

Discussion with the staff concerned

Arrange a meeting with the staff involved and explain the following:

- What the purpose of the structured group discussion(s) is, for example, to identify management task areas the staff feel could be managed more effectively if the teachers had the opportunity of some management development.
- How it will be organized.
- What the managerial tasks in the school are (see Table 1.1, p. 6).
- What is management development (see Chapter 1).

Ask the teachers to think about and write down three managerial task areas they feel could be handled more effectively if the staff responsible had some management development and training, and which they feel are priorities. Ask the teachers in the group to hand in their responses to you a few days later.

Collect the responses and record them on a master sheet to be presented at the next meeting.

A second discussion with the same group of staff a few days later

Hold a further meeting, present the results and encourage teachers to discuss each one briefly. This should not only clarify what each item actually means, but it should also enable you to identify responses that all seem to be addressing the same need, for example, concern that meetings for heads of department are not very effective; that heads of department and heads of year don't exchange enough information; and that main professional-grade teachers without posts of responsibility are frequently unclear about what is happening. All these could relate to the management of the communication and decision-making structures. Through discussion it should be possible to reduce the responses into a number of linked groups.

You may reach an agreement that one area of need is the best one to tackle but if not, proceed to a vote. Ask the teachers to vote for two or three tasks they feel could most usefully be worked on this year, for example:

Managerial task areas to work on this year

1. Collaboration between heads of department.
2. Allocation of managerial tasks between deputies.
3. School's links with the community.

Tally the results by allocating three points to the first choice, two to the second and one to the third. Check that everyone is happy with the final decision. Once you start working on the priority area (stage 3) you can explore exactly who needs what kind of support to learn to carry out these tasks more effectively.

Option 3: Interviews and Appraisals with Individual Members of Staff

You may not yet have a formal system for teacher appraisal but, nevertheless, would like to identify the management development needs of individual teachers. One way of doing this is to conduct informal but structured interviews with staff on a one-to-one basis. In contrast to an appraisal interview, these discussions would start with the teacher's perceptions of what he or she required in management training. The list of managerial tasks (Table 1.1) could be used to provide a framework for the discussion. This option was used in several schools, for example, 'The headteacher met with each member of staff individually and discussed their careers to date, their hopes and career prospects for the future and how the school and the LEA could assist in their general management

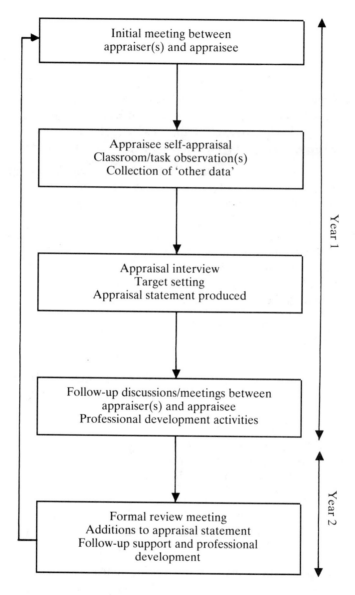

Figure 3.1   Components in the appraisal process

development'. 'Job descriptions have been prepared and are being discussed with permanent staff.'

A more sophisticated approach to individual needs diagnosis is the method proposed for appraisal, following the Teacher Appraisal Pilot Schemes, which is summarized in Figure 3.1. This draws upon a wide range of information, including self-appraisal and observation of a managerial task (e.g. chairing a meeting).

A detailed account of this approach is to be found in the handbook on appraisal in secondary schools (McMahon and Wallace, forthcoming – see Appendix I).

Option 4: Headteacher Selects Priority Area(s)

As the key manager in the school, the headteacher may feel that he or she is the only person with a wide enough knowledge of what is happening to be able to identify managerial task needs. If the head decides on a 'do-it-yourself' approach, we suggest that he or she adopts the following procedure:

1. Use the survey sheet (see option 1, above) as a guide. Think through which managerial task areas you feel it would be useful to work on this year, note the reasons for your choice and consider what the implications of this decision are.
2. Once you have come to a decision about which managerial task area(s) should be worked on this year, check it out with colleagues directly affected and any outsider, for example, LEA adviser for management development/ secondary adviser. Then consult and inform your colleagues on the staff about your decision in the way you feel is most appropriate.

This 'do-it-yourself' approach is probably the easiest but it runs the risk of being the one least likely to gain staff support and commitment.

Step 5: Decide on Strengths and Weaknesses of the School's Existing Management Development Provision

By this stage you should have gathered two types of information:

1. Some agreement about the managerial task areas where individuals or groups of teachers consider they need support to carry out the tasks more effectively.
2. An overview of the opportunities for management development that exist in the school already.

Try to synthesize these two sets of information and, in discussion with senior colleagues (and the management development core team), see if you can identify:

- aspects of the current policy and ongoing management development programme that are satisfactory and should be maintained;
- any unsatisfactory features of the ongoing management development programme and areas where it is not meeting needs; and
- which of these features (areas) should be dealt with as a specific priority project in the short (e.g. this year) or medium term (e.g. next two years) and which can be dealt with in the long term (e.g. five years).

You may well need to agree some criteria for assessing the effectiveness of your present programme but do not spend too long reaching your decision. The main aim is to reach some consensus about what you should work on first. For example, the fact that there is an induction programme for all new staff who join the school is almost certainly a strength – even though it may not be very good. If heads of department have no clear job descriptions and have never received any management training, this may well be regarded as a priority that should take precedence over the need to improve the induction programme.

Step 6: Agree a Step-by-Step Strategy for Achieving Systematic Management Development

Finally, you need to pull all the information together and decide what you are going to do in the year ahead. Review the short- and medium-term priorities you identified and consider how much time you should allocate to each. There are two important considerations to bear in mind. First, that the existing programme (e.g. induction for all teachers new to the school) will have to be maintained and this will take time. Second, that your immediate priorities should not necessarily be whole-school ones. It may be advisable to try to achieve a balance between tackling whole-school needs, group needs (e.g. reviewing the communication process, training all heads of department in interviewing techniques prior to the introduction of appraisal) and individual needs (e.g. specific training for an individual teacher in some aspect of interpersonal skills).

Some thought should be given to the time and financial resource implications of work in these priority areas. You will almost inevitably identify more priority areas than you can tackle in the short term. It could well be counter-productive to attempt to do too much – far better to do one or two things well and gain staff support for these than to have several initiatives uncompleted. Once you have a broad idea of what you are aiming to achieve in the long term, then you can move towards this over a number of years.

Finance will also have to be considered. It is often possible to undertake a great deal of management development in school at minimal cost but undoubtedly some activities will require funding. Even school-based activities may require cover if they take place during class-contact time. This has implications for supply-cover arrangements and for pupils' work. If the school has its own in-service budget the decision you have to take is comparatively straightforward – namely, what proportion of the total staff-development budget should be spent on management development? If the bulk of the INSET funds are held centrally by the LEA or allocated to consortia of schools then the school INSET co-ordinator will have to argue for funds in these other arenas.

Finally, consult appropriate colleagues (e.g. head, INSET co-ordinator) about your recommendations for priority work in the short and long term and use their advice to help you decide on next steps.

4

PRIORITY PROJECTS:
REVIEW AND ACTION PHASES

The purpose of the initial review (discussed in the previous chapter), was to identify a number of priority areas for the management development programme and to agree a strategy for working on these over a three-to-five-year period. We have decided to label each of your priorities a priority project and we have assumed that at least one person will undertake responsibility for investigating what kind of management development activities are required to meet needs identified in the priority area, and then mounting an appropriate programme of activities in school. Accordingly, this chapter is mainly addressed to the project leader, who may or may not be the school management development co-ordinator, and the other teachers who are involved in work on the priority project. The questions in the chapter focus on three key phases in a priority project (see Checklist 4.1):

1. The review phase, when the topic/issue is investigated in some detail and recommendations for action are produced.
2. The action phase, when the recommendations are put into practice.
3. The assessment or evaluation phase, when a decision is taken about whether or not the specific action or activity should be made a permanent feature of the school policy or programme.

The length of time allocated to a priority project will depend on the complexity of the issue. However, you should aim to have produced your action plan and, ideally, to have started implementing it within a term. In some instances you may be able to move into action more quickly.

Steps 1, 2 and 3 refer to the review phase and steps 4, 5 and 6 to the action phase.

*Checklist 4.1   Stage 3: priority projects, review and action phases –
key steps for the project leader and school management
development co-ordinator*

Step 1

Plan the review phase.

Tasks

1. Check why this topic was selected as a priority, decide how you should start on the project and what working methods should be employed.
2. Identify the people inside and outside the school who should be involved or consulted or from whom information might be gathered.
3. Draw up a timetable for the project.

Step 2

Clarify present policy/practice on the review topic.

Tasks

In consultation with the individual/group concerned:

1. establish, through document searches, interviews and observation, what is present policy and practice on the topic;
2. clarify what the precise management development needs in this area appear to be; and
3. decide upon criteria and procedures for assessing the effectiveness of present policy and practice and apply these.

Step 3

Assess and recommend.

Tasks

1. Judge the extent to which present practice is meeting identified needs.
2. Consider how identified but unmet needs might be dealt with.
3. Draw up your recommendations for action and check their feasibility and acceptability with those potentially affected and involved.
4. Consider whether you should inform/consult anyone, for example, governing body, LEA adviser, LEA INSET co-ordinator, about your action plans.

Step 4

Plan the action phase.

Tasks

1. Consider how you should start the action phase, what working methods might be employed and how the action can be evaluated.
2. Agree who should be responsible for organizing/running each part (or all) of the planned action.
3. Check what resources will be required for each activity and see that they are available.
4. Draw up a detailed timetable for the action phase of the project.

Step 5

Move into action.

Tasks

1. Implement the action plan.
2. Monitor the action (i.e. 'keep an eye on' what is happening).

Step 6

Assess and report on the action phase.

Tasks

1. Review any evaluation data or reports.
2. Judge the extent to which the action phase met its original aims and note any unintended consequences.
3. Agree your main conclusions and recommendations.
4. Check their feasibility and acceptability with those potentially affected and involved.

5. Finalize your conclusions about the action phase and
   - present them to the headteacher; and
   - present them to other appropriate people, for example, staff, governors, LEA adviser.

The Review Phase

Step 1: Plan the Review Phase

As a first step remind yourself why this topic/area was selected as a priority. You will need to look back at the information collected during the initial review stage. If some of the teachers filled in a questionnaire at that time, their written comments may provide a starting-point, otherwise you must rely on comments made in discussion or informal interviews. The priority may appear relatively straightforward (e.g. to improve preparation and follow-up support for teachers attending external management courses) or be much more nebulous (e.g. to help heads of department become better managers).

Examples of priority areas identified in the schools we worked with were:

- the management of time;
- how to minimize interruptions without becoming inaccessible and thus negating the objective of improving communications;
- how to develop better knowledge and understanding of, and to utilize more of, the time-saving equipment relating to modern computing and communication technology;
- the management of material resources; and
- how to improve the general managerial skills of middle managers.

If necessary, check quickly to see if others agree with your perception of why this area is a priority and how you should work on it. Then identify the people who are directly concerned with this area/task and who will therefore be the target group for management development. Depending on how many there are, some or all of them should form a small project review team with you. In some instances (e.g. management development for the deputy headteachers) only the senior management team may be directly involved, in others (e.g. managing communication) it may be one-third of the staff. However, there is plenty of evidence that people are more likely to accept a particular change if they have had an opportunity to influence it and to develop a sense of ownership about it; hence the need to ensure that if it is not possible for everyone relevant to join the review team at least their views can be represented. In discussion with the project review team try to identify any key issues you think you should focus upon.

Decide whom else inside or outside the school should be consulted. For example, if you are concerned about improving communication you may want to consult the dinner supervisor, caretaker and chairperson of the governors as well as members of staff. Finally, draw up a draft timetable for the review stage. It will be hard to do this precisely but it is a good idea to agree a date when you will produce your recommendations and to agree when any meetings should take place. A timetable is a good discipline and it should help you to clarify exactly what you can and cannot do. Aim for a thorough review in a realistic timescale (e.g. probably not more than half a term).

Step 2: Clarify Present Policy/Practice in the Review Topic/Area

The suggestions at this stage are to:

- establish through a variety of means what the present policy/practice in this area is;
- clarify what the precise management development needs in this area are; and

- decide on criteria and procedures for assessing the effectiveness of current policy and practice and apply these.

These suggestions may or may not appear straightforward in practice. If, for instance, the priority is to provide some management development and training for heads of subject departments, the reasons why this area was selected as a priority may be:

- unease on the part of some senior and more junior teachers that the heads of department were not managing their staff especially well;
- concern on the part of the head that the heads of department competed rather than collaborated with each other;
- department heads themselves requesting management development and training to enable them to cope with new responsibilities (e.g. for appraisal).

The review team would probably include some heads of department and you might all agree that the focus for your work should be to clarify the managerial responsibilities of the heads of department and to introduce some management development opportunities for them.

We suggest that you begin by clarifying the present provision of management development for this group. You may be able to do this very quickly by discussion, or you may want to interview one or two heads of department. For example, these management development opportunities might already be in place:

- Job descriptions, albeit somewhat inadequate, exist.
- The head and deputies hold a regular monthly meeting with heads of department in which issues of departmental management are often discussed.
- LEA guidelines exist for heads of department in particular subject areas.
- The LEA organizes INSET courses on the role and responsibilities of heads of department for which individuals are free to apply.
- One department head is known to be an excellent manager and would be pleased to share his or her expertise.

This would provide a good foundation on which to build.

Once you have clarified what the existing level of provision is, you should try to identify what the precise management development needs are. A variety of means can be used for this purpose. For instance, the teachers concerned could be individually interviewed, could complete a short questionnaire, could share their views about needs in a group discussion, etc. External perspectives can also be fed in. For example, the LEA may have given clear guidance on the responsibilities of heads of department; the head and senior management team may also have suggestions to feed into the discussion; and there could even be an input from HMI if they have visited the school recently. Remember that needs may be different from wants – the head and senior management team may feel that the heads of department have needs (e.g. to improve communication skills) they have not identified for themselves. Similarly, individual wants may be regarded as less urgent when viewed against the needs of the school. By collecting a range of views and opinions, the review team will be in a better position to decide what the key needs are.

Needs for new knowledge or particular skills may be reasonably easy to identify. For instance, heads of department may require some specific training if they are to assume a greater responsibility for financial management when more control for this is devolved to the school; they may also require training in classroom observation and in conducting a professional interview or dialogue on the introduction of teacher appraisal.

We suggest that, once you have clarified existing practice and identified needs, you assess how far the practice is meeting needs. You may have to draw up some criteria for this purpose. For instance, one group of teachers identified these features of good managerial practice in schools:

- Managers leading by example.
- Recognizing the value of teamwork, regardless of the personalities involved.
- Sensitivity to the needs of staff and showing concern as a colleague and friend.
- Offering encouragement (especially to take ownership of decisions), support and building confidence.
- Recognition (valuing people and their contribution).
- Ability to listen to others.
- Emphasis on all staff having responsibility for good personal relationships.
- Encouraging a continual exchange of views among staff.
- Sharing pleasant and unpleasant tasks.
- Being able to lead/persuade, train and instruct people.

If you felt it would be desirable if the heads of department behaved in this way, then you might use these points as criteria for assessing the effectiveness of an external course (e.g. did it give heads of department any practice in team-building?).

Step 3: Assess and Recommend

The suggestion here is that you judge the extent to which present practice is meeting identified needs, that you consider how unmet needs might be dealt with and that you draw up some recommendations for action. Let us follow through the example of management development for heads of department. If you agree that the qualities listed above are all desirable ones and that existing management development provision for heads of department does little to promote them, you must consider what management development activities would be more appropriate. A starting-point might be to consider what opportunities can be provided within the school, many of which will be at little or no cost. Examples might be:

1. the head clarifying job descriptions and discussing with heads of department what their managerial responsibilities are;

2. providing opportunities for heads of department to broaden their knowledge of school management by:

- participating in job selection and interviewing procedures;
- attending, as observer, a senior management team meeting; and
- shadowing a head of house/year for a few days.

Consider then what in-service opportunities are available within the LEA. It may be possible for a consortium of schools to sponsor a programme on team-building skills, or indeed the school may be able to identify a consultant who would provide some school-based training. (The directory of management development activities listed in Appendix I – Wallace, 1986 – is a source of ideas here.) Points to bear in mind when deciding upon a particular course of action are as follows:

- How appropriate is it, given what you want to achieve?
- What are the advantages and disadvantages of this particular strategy?
- How much time will a particular activity require?
- Can individuals or groups engage in it without external help?
- What financial resources are likely to be required?
- How suitable is it, given the previous experience of the group?
- How easy or difficult will it be to implement?
- What are the possible unintended consequences?
- How compatible is it with the school's development and in-service plan?
- What is the risk of things going wrong?

Once a list of recommendations for action have been produced their feasibility and acceptability need to be checked with those potentially concerned. Where appropriate, other people, for example, school adviser, INSET co-ordinators in neighbouring schools, may need to be consulted.

The Action Phase

The action phase of a project can be very exciting and rewarding but it can also be problematic. Without careful planning even an activity or change that has general staff support can go wrong. There are three broad steps at this stage:

Step 4 – plan the action phase.
Step 5 – implement/carry out the action.
Step 6 – assess the effectiveness of the action.

Step 4: Plan the Action Phase

It is likely that the teachers who formed the review team will also be responsible for implementing the action, but this will not invariably be the case. If new people are given this responsibility then they will obviously need careful briefing in advance. It may be possible to begin some activities almost immediately;

others, however, will have to wait until time or money become available – hence the need to see how management development can be fitted into the overall school staff-development and in-service programme. Look again at the range of management development activities listed in Table 1.2 (p. 7) and Tables 4.1 and 4.2. These distinguish between on-the-job, close-to-the-job and off-the-job activities. It is likely that your planned activities fall into the same categories. You will need to draw up a flexible plan and timetable for the various activities. For instance, if one suggestion is that someone should be sent on an LEA course (e.g. on using computers as a management tool) and that he or she should then run a school-based course to disseminate this knowledge to the other heads of department, arrangements will have to be made to:

- select the appropriate person;
- support his or her application for the course;
- provide preparatory briefings and support;
- arrange a de-briefing after the course;
- make arrangements for the school-based programme to disseminate the information learned.

Table 4.3 may help you to plan a range of activities. Activities that are on the job or close to it and that, therefore, probably take place in the classroom or school may be simpler to organize. You may be able to recommend that individual teachers arrange their own time for the activity (e.g. a head of department asks a colleague to observe a departmental meeting and to give feedback about it afterwards). Individual teachers can be asked to take on responsibility for their own self-development activities. They may find Checklist 4.2 a useful planning aid.

Step 5: Move into Action

A key point to remember at this stage is that plans should not become a strait-jacket but should remain reasonably flexible and adaptable. The activities can be monitored as they are taking place, and modified in the light of feedback from participants and to take account of changing circumstances. Monitoring means, in the first instance, checking to see that events that are supposed to happen do take place as planned. You need to keep an informal eye on activities to see if there are any unintended consequences or if problems arise that need to be sorted out.

The action stage is arguably the most important one since it is here that development and change can really occur as particular teachers participate in management development activities. The case studies in Chapter 6 illustrate what the action phase looked like in two schools.

Step 6: Evaluate and Report on the Action Phase

Michael Eraut and his colleagues, writing about the evaluation of INSET (Eraut,

Table 4.1   Externally provided off-the-job management development activities

---

A focus on management development might highlight the need for a different type of in-service course. The management development programme in one LEA included these courses, which are open to headteachers and senior staff.

● Advanced reading techniques	2 days
● Assertiveness	3 days
● Change-agent roles and skills for line managers	3 days
● Coping with change	2 days
● Effective speaking and presentation	2 days
● Equal opportunities 1: sex equality in employment	1 day
● Equal opportunities 2: race relations	1 day
● Finance for the non-financial manager	1 day
● Leadership	1 day
● Making meetings matter	1 day
● Motivation of staff	1 day
● Practical management skills	3 days
● Stress management: an introduction	1 day
● Time management	1 day
● Preparing for retirement	2 days

Table 4.2   Some ideas for management self-development activities

---

1. *Conducted by an individual*
   - Self-development exercises, e.g. time analysis, stress management
   - Private study in relation to the job
   - Action research into own performance

2. *Conducted with colleague(s) in school*
   - Two-way informal feedback – critical friendship
   - Exchanging tasks with preparation and feedback

3. *Conducted with teachers from other schools*
   - Shadowing colleague in the same position at work
   - Informal network (e.g. between deputy headteachers in part of the LEA)
   - Hotline – for administrative information
   - Focused visits to schools with mutual feedback
   - Action-learning set (e.g. with other headteachers)
   - Exchange of ideas and experience about specific tasks
   - Combined in-service meetings for heads, deputies or other teachers
   - Exchange jobs

4. *Conducted with external consultant*
   - Outsider, for example, adviser, observes a particular management activity (e.g. staff meeting) and gives feedback
   - Support groups (e.g. heads) linked to teachers' centre with central facilitator
   - Trainer gives in-school feedback and support with a particular task at intervals over a term

Table 4.3   Planning management development activities

				Resources required					
Activity	Time	Place	Materials	Supply cover	People expertise	Money	Other?	High/low risk	Pay-off

E.g. time
analysis

Checklist 4.2   Planning self-development activities

1. What is the activity and what does it involve doing?
2. What is its purpose?
3. Does the learning process involved match my view about how I learn?
4. What resources are needed and are these readily available?
5. How can I obtain any resources I need that are not readily available?
6. If other people are involved, what sort of working agreement do we need?
7. What is the most valuable potential outcome of the activity?
8. What are the risks and are these worth taking?
9. Are there any safeguards that would make a successful outcome more likely?
10. How much preparation and follow-up are required?
11. How does the activity fit in with my regular work?
12. How might the activity affect my colleagues in the school?
13. How may the activity be evaluated?

Pennycuick and Radnor, 1988, p. 12) defined it as follows: 'Evaluation is a) the collection, analysis, interpretation and reporting of evidence, b) about the nature, the impact and the value of the entity being evaluated, c) with due attention to concerns and issues identified by the various interested parties'.

They distinguish between administrative monitoring, professional monitoring and professional review as follows:

> Administrative monitoring: confines itself to budgets, attendance and administrative procedures of INSET and the staffing, facilities and throughput of institutions.
> Professional montoring: is concerned with customer satisfaction and with qualitative aspects of INSET processes. Were activities provided and received as planned? What strengths and weaknesses were perceived at the time? Were there any suggestions for improvements?

Professional review: goes beyond monitoring to ask more fundamental questions and to examine the assumptions which underpin practice. Some of these concern programme aims, rationales, long term impact and value. Others involved consideration of alternative policies and the re-assessment of priorities.

(*Ibid.*)

If we apply these definitions to management development, it follows that you would monitor and evaluate the action at this stage (administrative and professional monitoring), and that the professional review would take place in stage 5, which we have called the overview and re-start.

A key decision at the outset is to decide what you want to evaluate, how to do it and to agree a target date for considering the evaluation findings. You will need to agree what the evaluation should focus upon. Should it be confined to an examination of what happened and what participants and others felt about it, or should it also include an assessment of the impact of the activity on subsequent management performance? For example, if the activity to be evaluated was a school-based course for heads of department on how to chair a meeting, is it sufficient to know how the activity went and whether the participants felt it was beneficial, or should some attempt be made to judge whether or not there has been any improvement in individual performance? This second task is more difficult but in the long term may be more worth while (see Checklist 4.3).

It may be harder to decide on criteria against which to judge the effectiveness of what you are doing, especially if it is something completely new. You can become more rigorous as you become more skilled or experienced. For instance, in the first year of a scheme for staff-appraisal interviews, it may be sensible to concentrate on the process: is the 'right' type of information being collected, how is the interview being handled, etc.? At a later stage you might want to examine whether or not the appraisal process is having any impact on individual performance.

If you decide to evaluate the effectiveness of a particular activity and its impact on subsequent behaviour, you will need to agree on some criteria you can apply. For example, if the management development activity was intended to train a group of heads of department and deputies to chair and report back on meetings more effectively, what might these criteria be?

- That meetings now finish on time?
- That issues are resolved with less conflict and bad feeling?
- That written reports on meetings are clearer and more precise?
- That the deputy heads of department generally seem more confident about this aspect of their role?

Possible ways of assessing the effectiveness of the activity would be:

- asking the people directly concerned to complete a short questionnaire and to give their professional judgement about the value and practical usefulness of the training they received;
- asking a colleague head or deputy to observe and make notes on a few meetings before, during and after the training and then to make an assessment

Checklist 4.3   Key evaluation issues to consider at the planning stage

1. What is the purpose of the evaluation?

   - To improve/develop the programme?
   - To prepare a report on what has been achieved?

2. Who needs the information and why?

   - The teachers who participated in the activity?
   - The management development co-ordinator?
   - The whole-school staff?
   - The LEA advisers and officers?
   - The school governors?
   - The parents?

3. What will be evaluated?

   - Participant satisfaction with the activity?
   - The extent to which the original aims were achieved?
   - The effectiveness of each activity?
   - The impact of the management development programme on teacher attitudes and expertise?
   - The impact of the programme on the performance of individual teachers?
   - The cost in terms of human and financial resources?

4. Who will carry out the evaluation?

   - A teacher or group of teachers?
   - The management development co-ordinator?
   - The head?
   - An LEA adviser?
   - An independent evaluator (e.g. a teacher on secondment)?

5. How will the information be collected?

   - An analysis of documents and reports?
   - Questionnaires to staff? Others?
   - Interviews: structured or unstructured?
   - Written reports by participating teachers?
   - Observation of participants during the activity?
   - Observation of participants working with their colleagues afterwards?

6. What will happen to the information collected?

   - Will it be confidential to the evaluator and participants?
   - If not, who will have access to it?

- Will it be used as the basis of a verbal or written report?
- Who will receive any final report?
- How may the findings be used to improve aspects of the management development programme?

7. What resources will be needed?

- Time?
- Secretarial assistance?
- Supply cover?
- Money?

8. When and where will the evaluation processes be carried out?

based on as much factual information as possible – about whether or not there had been improvements in their performance, chairing, reporting back, etc.;
- inviting an external consultant to observe and report on how meetings were conducted before and after training; and
- checking whether the department business seems to be handled more efficiently.

Once you have assessed the effectiveness of the action phase, reach some conclusions and, having checked them with the appropriate people, present them to the head (if he or she is not the management development co-ordinator) and other teachers, as appropriate.

These conclusions can then be fed into the next stage, overview and re-start.

5

OVERVIEW AND RE-START

The suggestions in this chapter are directed to the headteacher, the school management development co-ordinator (if not the head) and members of the core team. They are intended to help you to review the position of the school management development policy and programme periodically, and to decide its future direction (see Checklist 5.1). Since you will have to review your whole staff-development and in-service programme each year in order to prepare a bid for in-service funding under the terms of the LEA Training Grants Scheme (LEATGS) it may be sensible to make a professional reveiw (in Eraut, Penny-cuick and Radnor's 1988 terms) of the management development policy and programme at the same time. However, you may feel – at least at the outset – that this is better done less frequently (e.g. once every two years).

Step 1: Plan the Overview

The head is probably the person best placed to decide when it would be appropriate to review the overall management development policy and programme. The exercise need not involve many people, though it is likely that the senior management team and the school INSET co-ordinator would need to be consulted. However, the management development co-ordinator should ensure that each person involved in the meeting should have access to data that will enable them to come to an informed decision about the programme – hence the need for summary reports on the ongoing activities and the priority project(s).

Step 2: Review the Strengths and Weaknesses of the School Management Development Policy and Programme

The main question to consider here is the extent to which the management development policy and programme is now meeting school needs. Refer back to

Checklist 5.1   Stage 4: overview and re-start – key steps for the management development co-ordinator, the core team and the head

---

Step 1

Plan the overview.

Tasks

1. Agree the procedures for the overview, for example, who should be involved, date for the meeting, timetable.
2. Prepare a summary report on the current stage of progress of:

   (a) the ongoing programme; and
   (b) the specific priority project including any evaluation reports.

3. Distribute this summary report before the meeting.

Step 2

Review the strengths and weaknesses of the school management development policy and programme.

Tasks

1. Decide whether the ongoing programme is now meeting your needs.
2. Decide whether the new activities/features arising from priority projects that you have been integrating into the programme should be maintained.
3. Decide what action to take about any outstanding priority projects.

Step 3

Decide on the usefulness of the NDC approach as a way of achieving systematic management development.

Tasks

1. Review the extent to which the main stages and the particular working techniques recommended were actually used.
2. Identify the advantages and disadvantages of this approach in your school.
3. Decide whether this approach should be dropped, continued or adapted.

Step 4

Next steps and possible re-start.

Tasks

1. Draft a summary report on the conclusions from steps 2 and 3.
2. Distribute this report to the appropriate people and seek their agreement on the conclusions and recommendations.
3. If you are going to use this approach again (or an adapted form of it), decide whether:

   (a) you need to conduct another initial review; or
   (b) you can move straight into another priority project (stage 3).

Table 1.3 (p. 10). Where are you now and what level had you hoped to reach by this stage? Consider whether changes introduced as a result of a priority project should be maintained. For instance, you may have decided that each term one of the meetings for heads of department should be used for development and training – do you want to continue this next year? Another point to consider is whether there have been any changes in the school that raise new priorities, for example, replacement of key members of staff, introduction of a new teaching programme. If priority projects have been identified but not yet tackled, decide what you are going to do about this.

Step 3: Decide on the Usefulness of the NDC Approach as a Way of Achieving Systematic Management Development

The suggestions in this handbook are intended to help you establish a more systematic approach to management development. A step-by-step approach has been suggested in which you make an initial review of needs, identify one or more priority areas for review and development and work on these in the first instance. The central notion is that you can work on different priority areas over a number of years. Consider first how closely you have followed the suggested procedure and then reflect on the advantages and disadvantages of this approach.

Questions you might ask are as follows:

● Did the co-ordinator have sufficient time to do the job?
● Did something occur that upset your planning, for example, a period of teacher action, an LEA innovation to which you had to respond?
● Were staff in school sufficiently aware of what was happening and were they adequately consulted?
● Were you able to fit work for the priority projects into the normal cycle of the school year?
● What were the benefits of this work to strengthen the provision of management development?
● What were the disadvantages of working on management development?

Undoubtedly you will be able to identify areas for improvement if you were to continue working in this way and perhaps tackle another priority project. If things have not worked as well as you hoped, try to identify what caused the problems: was the systematic approach suggested inappropriate, or was there some other cause (e.g. the management development co-ordinator left the school half way through the year to move to another post)? You need to reach some conclusion about whether or not to continue with this approach.

Step 4: Next Steps and Possible Re-Start

Once you have completed the overview you need to decide on next steps. You may decide to concentrate for a time on sustaining the central ongoing programme. You may decide that there are no immediate priorities to tackle or you may decide to work on another priority project. Your decision will probably be influenced by priorities highlighted in the school development plan and the in-service programme. If you decide to tackle another priority project you will probably be able to move straight into it as, unless there have been big changes in the school, you will only need to conduct a review every two or three years.

Look again at Figure 1.1 (p. 11) to remind yourself of the various stages in the process. We suggest that your overall conclusions at this stage should be fed into discussions about the whole-school INSET needs.

You will need to consider how you can best fit work on a priority project in management development into the school timetable for the year. Questions we assume you will want to think about are as follows:

- How can you make some time available for the management development co-ordinator – should you do this when the timetable is drawn up?
- How are you planning to allocate directed time? Will there be some flexibility that would enable teachers to join review teams, etc., without too much difficulty?
- Does the school have its own INSET budget? If it does, how much money is available and what proportion of it can be allocated to management development?
- If the school has to submit bids for in-service activities to the LEA or to a consortium, when does this have to be done and when do you hear whether or not your bid has been successful?

6

SCHOOL MANAGEMENT DEVELOPMENT: TWO CASE STUDIES

Case Study 1

Introduction

This case study is about one of the schools we worked with. It describes how the head and staff in a school that had already undertaken some work on management development decided to strengthen this provision by working on a priority project. The topic they selected was managing the school communication and decision-making structures. The case study is based on reports written by the headteacher and the deputy head who shared the management development co-ordinator role.

The Context

The school is an 11–18 comprehensive with 1,230 students and 77 staff. One of the deputy headteachers has responsibility for staff development, and a well-established programme of activities, which includes a number of school-focused initiatives, is in place. There is a staff handbook that contains the aims of the school, detailed job descriptions for all staff in their varying academic and pastoral roles and details of the school's committee structure. The school has a policy of encouraging all staff to take advantage of INSET courses and increasingly these take account of the management role of teachers. The head feels that the senior staff of the school are all aware of their management role and says that a significant degree of responsibility has been delegated not only to senior staff but also to 'middle management'.

Stage 1: Getting Started

Initially the headteacher was asked by an LEA adviser if he would be interested in collaborating with the LEA and the NDC to work on management development. The head read the suggestions contained in the handbook and expressed interest. He said he believed that any initiative that enabled the school to be a more effective unit should be examined carefully and adopted, if at all possible – though he recognized that there was already a considerable amount of provision for management development in the school. He then had a discussion about management development with the deputy headteacher and other members of the senior staff, and all agreed that it would be valuable to do some more work in this area. The main concern expressed was about the time such work might require. The head and one of the deputies decided to share the job of school management development co-ordinator and the other members of the senior staff formed a core team.

Comment

One point worth emphasizing here is that the staff were prepared to work to strengthen their existing good provision of management development – they were not complacent about what had already been achieved.

Stage 2: The Initial Review

The core team decided that all the staff should have an opportunity to contribute to the decision about what the priority topic for management development should be. They discussed how the question should be introduced in order to obtain optimum response from the staff, and a number of ideas were put forward. Finally, they agreed that the staff should be told about management development as a group rather than piecemeal, and that they should then be invited to complete the survey sheet (a modified version of Example 3.1, p. 37). The head persuaded the LEA to agree to a half-day school closure and at this stage he also approached the chairman of governors, gave him a copy of the handbook and obtained his support.

On the day appointed for the meetings, the staff were divided into seven discussion groups with ten teachers in each. It was decided that these groups would be cross-curricular, would be balanced in terms of status and would be chaired by heads of department or staff of equivalent status. The senior staff would act as 'consultants' entering the discussion groups at the half-way stage. The staff had all been given a copy of an information paper on management development to read in advance, and the group leaders had been briefed. The intention was that teachers would have an opportunity to talk about management development in their group and then would be given a survey sheet to complete in their own time. Things did not go entirely as planned. To start with, the meeting was taking place on a Friday in February and by lunchtime it was snowing heavily. During the morning the head had to issue the staff with the

LEA's response to proposed action by two of the teacher unions, and this had not been well received. It did not seem an auspicious time to launch a new initiative. In the afternoon the head spoke briefly about management development, emphasized the importance of the management role played by teachers and stated his considered belief that teachers have, by the very nature of their job, to be good managers. The staff then broke up into their discussion groups. The senior staff held a management meeting. The success of the discussion groups relied heavily on the quality of the chairmen: one ensured that staff were comfortable and that conversation was relaxed, another used it as an opportunity to criticize the senior staff of the school. When the senior staff joined the groups just after the halfway stage in discussions scheduled for one and a half hours, six were invited to stay and one was asked to leave after answering a few questions about management development and the survey sheet. The plenary session was short and provoked no major discussion.

A number of survey sheets were handed in that evening and the majority were returned by the time given on Monday morning. By an overwhelming margin, the two areas that were causing most concern were:

1. managing the school communication and decision-making structures; and
2. managing staff.

Many of the comments were very critical of the school's management and lacked positive suggestions. As far as the deputy (who was sharing the co-ordinator role) and the head were concerned, it was not a time for the sensitive, the thin-skinned or those who might react quickly. The head felt that while some of the criticism might well be justified, there was no doubt that events at the time had a distorting influence on the nature of the response and indeed on the strength of concern for the two areas chosen – which were both related to staff as opposed to students. The survey results were published in the weekly bulletin for staff.

Comment

Viewed with hindsight, it might have been advisable to allow more time to elapse between the staff discussion about management development and their completing the survey sheet. However, this experience does underline the importance of timing the introduction of a new initiative carefully. Because this was a collaborative project, the head felt under some pressure to get started quickly.

Stage 3: Priority Project – Review and Action Phases

This section focuses upon the first priority project – managing the school communication and decision-making structures. The head and deputy were mainly responsible for the review stage, though they checked things with other members of the core team when appropriate. The initial review had taken place in the first part of the spring term and they moved quickly into a detailed review of the priority area. They drew up two questionnaires, one on managing communication and the other on decison-making structures, which were issued and completed before Easter. Both questionnaires were issued to all staff and they were requested to give their views on present practice in a detailed and constructive manner. The head said that these questionnaires produced a useful response and that, although individual teacher's prejudices were still occasionally in evidence, their comments were generally more reflective, sensible and useful. He added that, in a staff of over 70, a number of directly conflicting views as to how things should be managed were to be expected, and one of the tasks would be to focus on those areas where there was a marked consensus.

Analysis of the questionnaire responses indicated that there were a number of areas where existing procedures could be improved. The following are some of the key points raised:

- Concern was expressed at the lack of information from the pastoral committee and, generally, staff seemed unaware of the nature and working of this body.
- There were complaints from tutors that they were not receiving the information they required for their form-tutor meetings.
- Staff briefing meetings were requested.
- Great variations were reported in the frequency and organization of departmental meetings.

Several suggestions were made about what would constitute good practice in these areas.

The head reported that considerable dissatisfaction was expressed at the lack of good management and commented that it was interesting to note the disparity between heads of departments (who felt they were running things efficiently) and members of those departments (who complained of lack of information and lack of consultation). He said that good practice was identified, the two main examples being form-tutor meetings and departmental meetings, where there was a variety of organization and frequency. Staff indicated that they expected these meetings to be frequent and to be well organized.

He added that, on the less positive side, the responses indicated a lack of understanding of the close relationship there has to be between taking a decision and accepting responsibility for that decision. Some staff obviously felt they should have a major decision-making role, although they were in no position to accept responsibility for decisions taken. There were also staff who assumed that, when they were consulted, their views would be accepted and were disappointed and somewhat cynical when they were not. Yet he felt that there would be times when an individual's opinion could not be accepted and when the majority view would be taken.

Action taken after the review in the summer term included the following:

- The pastoral committee began to issue better and fuller communications to the staff.
- Heads of department were given clear guidance about how they should conduct departmental meetings and how frequently they should be held; the

intention was to extend good practice in this area across all departments in the school.

- Two short briefing meetings for staff each week were introduced – these were solely for the dissemination of information.
- Heads of year were asked to organize formal meetings for their form tutors on a fortnightly basis; again the intention was to extend good practice across the school.
- Two working parties were set up to investigate two areas about which concern had been expressed but where no clear strategy for future action had emerged. The areas were staff meetings and cross-curricular links.
- The existing structures for communication and decision-making were clarified and staff were encouraged to use them.

Comment

The problem of how to manage communication in a large and complex organization is by no means an unusual one. This case study is a useful illustration of the issues that can arise in a school that seems to be running efficiently and effectively, and where the staff have already been working to improve their managerial skills. It is useful to reflect for a moment on who received management development in this instance. First, the work on the priority project was undoubtedly a powerful management development opportunity for the heads of department. It heightened their own awareness of their role as managers; their existing practices in staff management were held up to scrutiny and criticized; finally, agreement was reached about how they should best organize meetings and manage staff in their departments. Adopting the 'best-practice' model for departmental meetings would have meant quite a radical change in behaviour for some of the heads of department concerned. Clearly, the exercise heightened awareness of the managerial role of heads of year and established a model of good practice for communication with form tutors, which they were encouraged to adopt. The head and the deputy headteacher – who were jointly acting as school management development co-ordinators – received a considerable amount of practical experience while managing the whole priority project. Finally, it can be argued that all the staff benefited to some extent, and that the managerial capacity in the school was increased because communication structures were clarified and streamlined and everyone gained a better understanding of his or her responsibility for ensuring that the structures worked effectively.

Stage 4: Overview and Re-Start

The changes introduced during the action stage were monitored to check they were being implemented as planned. Further work continued on the two areas of staff meetings and cross-curricular links that had been highlighted for further investigation. The head said he believed that, despite any problems that had occurred, the work was having a beneficial effect on the school by heightening a realization of teachers' roles as managers. He made two further important points. First, that any review that does take place must be able to identify clearly faults in the system as distinct from an individual's operation of the system. Obviously if an individual manager within the system was operating inefficiently, it is the duty of the school management to improve that individual rather than to make major alterations in the management system. Second, that work on a priority project for management development should not prevent other initiatives taking place in the school.

Comment

It is useful to remind ourselves again that the ultimate aim of management development is to improve the teaching and learning processes: it is not an end in itself. Management development should be part of a school's staff-development programme and should aid the smooth running of the school – not hinder it. An important management task is to plan when management and staff development can best take place without causing too much disruption to the general life of the school.

Case Study 2

Introduction

This case study is also about one of the schools we worked with. It describes how the staff approached work on management development and is based on reports written by the headteacher, who was the management development co-ordinator, and members of the core team.

The case study illustrates the way in which a group of teachers interpreted the broad advice in the NDC handbook about how to work on a priority project. It is interesting in a number of respects. First, it shows how planning can be over-taken by events: the slow progress at the outset was influenced by factors outside any one person's control. Second, it demonstrates that some external support at the right time, in this case from an LEA adviser, can help a school to move forward. Finally, it demonstrates that, in practice, management development is not a discrete activity but is something that can have implications for the whole school. Here, it influenced the general staff-development programme and the curriculum.

The Context

The school is a larger 11–18 co-educational comprehensive. The school roll is approximately 1,400 and there are 87 members of staff. The school serves a mixed catchment area but has a large percentage of children with multi-racial backgrounds. The school is organized into an upper, middle and lower school, and each building is administered by one of three deputies. There is a well-defined system for academic and pastoral organization in place.

Stage 1: Getting Started

The initial stages of the project in the school were rather protracted for a number of reasons, largely outside anyone's control. The headteacher had decided to work on management development in collaboration with the NDC, and had identified a core team of seven members of staff ranging from the deputies to scale-two teachers. A series of consultative meetings was held with this group and then with the whole staff; one of the deputies was designated as school co-ordinator. The head interviewed members of the core team to clarify what their individual management development needs were, and steps were taken in response to this to increase the range of management development opportunities available within the school. Unfortunately at this stage, three things happened that severely hindered progress. The first and most significant was a worsening period of industrial action, which made it very difficult to hold meetings with staff and to initiate new activity. Then the school co-ordinator became ill and a key member of the senior staff left the school to take up an LEA post. Finally, there was a change of headteacher. This combination of factors meant that little happened for over a year.

However, shortly after the appointment of the new headteacher, the senior adviser (who was acting as LEA management development co-ordinator), called two meetings to discuss progress on management development at school level. The new head was interested in management development and, encouraged by the promise of LEA support, decided to start working on it again. In view of low teacher morale as a result of the action, he felt the priority area should be a topic with a specific time limit and should be something that would be of use to the school generally. He selected a core team of nine people (this group was finally reduced to six for a variety of reasons), representing teaching staff at all levels from those with only a few years' experience to the headteacher: 'The group represented the teaching areas of language, special education, science, humanities, maths, creative and domestic subjects. All staff involved saw the work as a way of developing management expertise at a number of levels within the school'.

Comment

The main reason we suggest that a school designates someone as management development co-ordinator is so that this person can sustain the momentum of the work in this area. Unless there is some contingency plan or the programme is already well established, problems may still arise if the co-ordinator is away for any length of time – but at least the likelihood of the work coming to an abrupt halt is reduced, especially if the LEA provides some external support.

Stage 2: The Initial Review

The headteacher decided to select the priority topic himself. Given that the initial discussions had been protracted but that little activity had as yet resulted, he felt that stages 1 and 2 should be curtailed and that work on the specific priority should start as soon as possible. Consequently he chose the topic, 'management of learning style/teaching strategy', as he felt this was at the very core of the profession's task. He felt this topic would not only allow management development in its many forms (e.g. the management of school policy, curriculum, staff, pupils, resources, relationships and the process of evaluation) but would also ensure a more effective use of the school's greatest resource, its teachers. The core team accepted the reasons for the decision and the work was begun. It started in November and the target was to complete it by the following July, the end of the school year.

Comment

Note that, though the headteacher identified the priority topic, he did consult the members of the core management development team and gain their agreement. We do suggest that the initial review should not last too long (e.g. not more than a term) and, given that matters had already been delayed, it was probably sensible of the head to identify the priority topic quickly.

Stage 3: Priority Project – Review and Action Phases

The team started its research by attempting to quantify what makes a successful lesson. Effective class management techniques were examined on the basis that if the atmosphere was not right then learning could not proceed.

They agreed on a number of key points and subsequently prepared a file of information on 'Preventative Approaches to Disruption', which was placed in the staffroom. The file contained advice and checklists on lesson organization and teaching skills. They then turned their attention to teaching strategies and decided that they should focus on innovative strategies rather than the traditional 'chalk-and-talk' approach. Techniques that had served the staff in the core team well, and that therefore might be of use to colleagues, were considered – as were those that were new. They felt it was particularly important that experimental approaches were attempted, if only to prove the point that a teacher should not fear or avoid change but rather assess and evaluate the new response required to meet changing pupil needs. They decided to use a variety of data-gathering methods:

1. They undertook a series of lesson observations (of each other and other colleagues), the main objective of which was to assess different learning styles, for example, practical lessons, open learning, oral lessons, group work and student-centred learning.
2. Staff who had been on relevant courses were consulted and other colleagues were invited to advise on specific areas.
3. Some members of the team attended relevant in-service courses and reported back on the key learning points.

Reflecting on the lesson observations later, the members of the core team made these comments about existing practice:

a. The teaching styles of those involved were varied, ranging from formal through to progressive, with some experimental techniques.
b. With regard to colleagues observing lessons, there was an initial degree of reservation, which was soon to be dispelled by what was later described as a 'positive experience'.
c. As a rule, all departments represented on the core team held meetings but the industrial climate at the time led to disruption of the normal patterns.
d. Not all departments had a specific policy on teaching methods. With the advent of GCSE, it was recognised that a more uniform approach within each subject would be necessary.
e. Generally it was the case that the production of departmental resources was not shared or organised.
f. Given the pressures of a 35 period teaching week, it was found to be not always possible to think through the aims of each individual lesson. After discussion it was agreed that most teachers absorbed the pressure, and that this was not a satisfactory solution. Department organisation which encouraged effective sharing of preparation of resources and structuring the workloads had to be the major way of reducing the pressures on the teacher.

In all about twenty hours was spent examining a range of teaching strategies. The core-team members discussed and assessed the information they had collected at a series of meetings and decided to produce a practical report for their colleagues on the staff. In all thirteen approaches were considered:

1. Classroom management: lesson observations.
2. Good classroom management and preventive approaches to disruption.
3. Supported self-study.
4. Open learning.
5. 'Study skills'.
6. Individualized learning packages and libraries.
7. Computers.
8. Technician/ancillary help across the curriculum.
9. School-based resources centre.
10. Support materials.
11. Display.
12. The role of video technology.
13. Resources in the local community.

A short account, approximately two sides of A4, was produced on each approach. This described what the strategy was, drew attention to departments in the school where it was being used, commented on the perceived advantages and disadvantages of the strategy and its relevance for particular groups, and, finally, suggested where teachers could get additional information and advice.

The action phase of the project had a number of specific outcomes:

1. Development for those staff who had been involved in the core team.

2. A practical handbook for the staff and a clear plan for subsequent in-service work on learning styles.
3. Specific recommendations for the LEA.

Comment

Class management techniques and teaching styles are often regarded as matters to be decided upon by each individual teacher. With the exception of probationary teachers, it is still rare for teachers to have their lessons observed, and senior and middle managers in schools frequently have not concerned themselves with the teaching styles adopted by the staff (except in the comparatively rare cases where a teacher is known to be having problems controlling the pupils). However, the introduction of a whole series of curriculum innovations (e.g. TVEE, GCSE, pupil profiling) means that new teaching techniques are required and the head and senior and middle managers cannot afford to ignore what goes on in the classroom. Indeed, they would be foolish to do so, since research evidence shows that taking a lead in these matters can result in school improvement.

More specific points illustrated in this section are:

● the core team agreed at the outset on criteria for effective class management;
● that information can be disseminated as the work progresses – everything does not have to be kept for a final report. Note that the team produced and disseminated information on 'preventative approaches to disruption' at an early stage in their work; and
● the value of making a detailed examination of existing practice, in this case by means of lesson observations and discussion. Once the team had gained some understanding of the way various departments dealt with teaching style, they were better placed to make recommendations for strengthening this aspect of a head of department's work.

Stage 4: Overview and Re-Start

The members of the core group completed a questionnaire towards the end of the summer term, as their work was concluding, to assess their views of what they had done. The analysis of this highlights a number of important issues.

What had they gained as managers from this exercise?

1. Watching colleagues at work was considered to be a valuable experience, from which a great deal was learned.
2. Observing colleagues helped to break down many negative barriers and encouraged the development of positive attitudes and the sharing of ideas. Additional benefits included cross-curricular experiences, which were found to be invaluable.
3. The general opinion was that there had not been an adequate opportunity to observe as many lessons as would have been desirable, and more time/cover should be made available in any future programme.

4. The group encountered many new methods, as detailed in the previous sections of this case study.
5. If the time had been available, there were many areas the group felt could have been studied. These included the experience of teaching in special education, the ethos of the extra-curricular approach and in-built assessment techniques.
6. There had been much value in meeting colleagues in the course of the work:

   (a) It had been a confidence-building exercise, improving relationships between individuals and departments.
   (b) It had enhanced communications leading to a greater degree of sharing ideas.
   (c) It had increased insight into the difficulties faced by others.

7. Although the group spent over twenty hours discussing aspects of learning styles, it was recognized that some issues had not been adequately assessed because of time constraints.
8. The group had developed a number of positive attributes – mainly an increase in self-confidence, self-evaluation and a degree of experimentation and flexibility.

What had (or would) they put into practice?

1. Many new techniques were used as the project progressed. Most members of the group improved the presentation of worksheets, which gave rise to a favourable response and corresponding increase in interest from the pupils.
2. It was unanimously felt that their personal class-teaching methods would continue to develop and improve as a result of a greater awareness of the skills and techniques presented to them.
3. The self-confidence of each member of the group improved, enabling individuals to try new approaches, assess them and, subject to modification, continue to develop them.

Finally, the team asked themselves: was the information worth disseminating? They agreed that it was, though they recognized that the response of colleagues to their work had been varied, extending from those who were totally unaware of its existence, to those who showed interest and were keen to see the results and to others who were sceptical. A range of methods for disseminating the information was suggested, the most popular and effective being INSET. Other possibilities included:

1. a written report;
2. a report via a heads of department meeting; and
3. cascading from committee members after further detailed training in their specific areas of interest.

The team recommended that departments should draw up a policy on resources that would ease and unify the production of materials. They also suggested that a staff library should be set up. Some specific recommendations for the LEA were also produced. These were that schools required and would benefit from:

- school-based, fully equipped resource centres;
- ancillary staff for reprographics;
- an adequate INSET budget;
- involvement of LEA advisers; and
- money to invest in resources as the need arose in response to the work in progress, for example, buy a book, etc.

Comment

The action phase of this project will extend over a number of years, formally through in-service training programmes and the provision of information packs about class management and teaching styles for the staff. Informally, it has resulted in more discussion about teaching methods, a greater willingness to experiment with new approaches and to share ideas – this new climate started with a small group of teachers but could spread far beyond them. In terms of management development, one of the most significant outcomes was probably the emphasis on, and greater clarity about, the role the head of department could adopt as mentor and guide to colleagues in the department on class management and teaching styles.

PART III
THE ONGOING MANAGEMENT
DEVELOPMENT PROGRAMME

In Part II we suggest how a school might strengthen its management development policy and programme by reviewing its existing provision, identifying a
number of priority projects and working on these systematically over a number
of years. In Part III we suggest how you might sustain management development
activities in school, whether or not you are working on priority projects.

There are two chapters in this section:

Chapter 7   Linking management and staff development.
Chapter 8   Supporting school management development.

Both chapters are addressed to all the teachers who have some involvement
with the management development programme. The audience for Chapter 8
could also include LEA advisers and any consultants working on school management development.

7
LINKING MANAGEMENT AND STAFF DEVELOPMENT

This chapter is addressed mainly to the headteacher, the school management development co-ordinator and the members of the senior management team. The definition of management development given in the first part of this handbook was that it was 'staff development for those teachers who have school management responsibilities'. In this chapter we want to consider how management development can be integrated and sustained as part of the overall school staff-development policy and programme. There is a sense in which it is just an additional dimension to this programme. Many teachers are likely to have managerial responsibility at some stage in their career and they need development and training for this in the same way that they need opportunities to update their subject knowledge and pedagogic skills. The balance of needs will alter as they progress through their careers. For example, the management development needs of a deputy head in a large secondary school are likely to be more pressing than those of a newly qualified teacher. Yet all main-scale teachers could probably benefit from a modicum of management training (e.g. on how to work as a member of a departmental team).

In Figure 1.1 the management development programme was set in the context of the whole-school INSET programme. Four stages were identified:

1. Review of management development needs within the annual school INSET planning cycle.
2. Inclusion of management development in the annual school and staff-development plan.
3. Implementation of the school and staff-development plan.
4. Evaluation of the school and staff-development plan.

In many schools this cycle is now tied to the LEA INSET planning cycle and programme and includes a specific management development component.

Whenever possible you should try to raise the general level of consciousness about school management, and help teachers to understand and to come to terms with their role as managers. This will help to establish the legitimacy and importance of the management development component in the overall in-service programme. Some specific suggestions you might consider are the following:

1. *Staff-appointment procedures*   Try to improve selection and appointment procedures, for example, by preparing up-to-date job descriptions, specifying what qualities and skills are required for the job, preparing detailed and useful information for candidates, briefing the interviewing panel, etc. A regular staff-appointment procedure could also be used as a management development exercise by, for example, involving a head of house who has never previously sat on an interviewing panel.

2. *In-service needs identification procedures*   If you are using some system for whole-school review or for identifying INSET needs (e.g. that of Capell, Mills and Poster, 1987), try to ensure that questions are asked about management development needs as well as needs relating to teaching, the curriculum, etc.

3. *Staff in-service days*   Each school now has five in-service days each year. Could one of these be allocated to management development activities? Can someone be given responsibility for organizing an in-service day as a specific management task and given feedback afterwards about their performance?

4. *Meetings*   Every school has numerous meetings for large and small groups of teachers and the staff as a whole. The potential of these meetings as management development activities could be enhanced if different people were given opportunities to chair the meetings in turn, and if, occasionally, the last few minutes of a meeting were used for a general de-briefing session about the way people felt it had gone. Neither of these things need obstruct the main agenda.

5. *Preparation and follow-up for teachers attending external courses*   The likelihood of teachers being able to apply learning acquired on a course when they are back in school is considerably enhanced if they receive preparation and follow-up support. Many schools have realized this and try to build this support into the staff-development programme. Teachers are encouraged to report on the course, to discuss it with colleagues and, where appropriate, may be given help to implement some new ideas. This preparation and follow-up would ideally be provided for people going on management courses as much as any other, even if the people in question are members of the senior management team.

6. *Staff library*   If the school in-service co-ordinator/professional tutor is building up a small library of books on staff development for staff use it would be useful to enhance this collection with some key works on management in schools and management development.

7. *Use 'in-house' expertise*   In every school large numbers of teachers carry out managerial tasks every day; some of them do them extremely well. Yet, because school management was for so long a rather covert activity in that it

was only spoken about when things went wrong, the expertise of these teachers went largely unnoticed. If management development gains greater prominence in the school, then teachers who are good managers can become 'trainers' for their colleagues. Numerous techniques can be adopted, ranging from formal seminars and talks to one teacher observing or 'shadowing' a colleague. Knowledge and expertise that can be shared in this way is not just technical (e.g. how to draw up a timetable) but can include people-management skills (e.g. resolving conflict between two parties, interviewing, giving honest feedback about performance).

8

SUPPORTING SCHOOL MANAGEMENT DEVELOPMENT

This chapter is mainly addressed to the head, the management development co-ordinator and members of the senior management team. It should also be relevant for the LEA adviser with responsibility for the school and any external consultants, industrialists, etc., who may become involved with the management development programme. There is a companion handbook (McMahon and Bolam, 1990a – see Appendix I) that suggests how an LEA can strengthen its LEA-wide provision of management development for headteachers and senior and middle managers in schools. In this chapter we will only refer to the kinds of external support that might help teachers to establish a school management development programme.

A great deal, possibly the bulk, of management development takes place on the job, in school and so it is right that it is essentially a matter for the head-teacher and his or her colleagues to arrange. Nevertheless, most schools would benefit from external support and advice at various stages. In the majority of cases this support will be provided by the LEA but occasionally it might be supplied by an external consultant or trainer.

Provide a 'Vision' for School Management

The LEA can make a valuable contribution by initiating and contributing to a debate about how schools might or should be managed. School management development programmes are intended to make individuals and groups of teachers better managers, but frequently the philosphies and values that under-pin such programmes are left implicit. A head may not share them with staff in the school, let alone with staff in other schools across the LEA. So, for instance, if the LEA advisers and officers feel that the head and deputy headteachers should operate as a very close team, that decisions should be taken in as open a manner as possible, that all teachers should have an opportunity to express their views on major items of school policy and that as many decisions as possible should be devolved to middle managers (e.g. heads of department and heads of year) – then these are issues they can put forward for discussion and debate. All have profound implications for the way teachers fulfil their managerial role and so for the management development programme.

Allocate Resources to Management Development

A very tangible form of support the LEA can provide is to allocate resources for management development. This would require them to earmark a proportion of the in-service budget for management development and training and to ensure that, whether the money was held centrally or was given to consortium and individual schools, it was spent on management training activities as intended.

Provide a Programme of Management Courses and Activities

We began this chapter by saying that a great deal of management development must take place in school, but this does not mean there is no room for the external course. Some forms of training (e.g. induction programmes for newly appointed headteachers) are much better done centrally, and courses that might be run at LEA level may well not be financially feasible in a consortium or an individual school. Ideally, the LEA would be able to mount a programme of short and longer management training courses and activities (e.g. action-learning groups) designed to meet identified management development needs.

Designate Someone as LEA Management Development Co-ordinator

Management development is a relatively new concept in education. When schools are just starting to build up their own management development programmes it can be very useful to have a named person to whom they can turn for advice and help. This person can take a leading part in providing all the other forms of support mentioned here.

Support for School Management Development Co-ordinators

In the early stages when schools are drawing up management development policies and extending their programme of activities, the LEA can provide several kinds of very practical help for school management development co-ordinators. To begin with an LEA adviser can recommend to the head that someone is designated as co-ordinator. Once a co-ordinator is in place an adviser can provide individual advice and suggestions for action during visits to the school, and he or she can also organize occasional meetings for all the co-ordinators in a particular group of schools or across the LEA. Such meetings can provide an invaluable opportunity for exchanging information and ideas. The LEA might even arrange some specific training for co-ordinators if this seemed necessary.

Provide Access to Materials

The LEA might establish a central information resources bank of management training materials that individual schools could use. Examples of such materials would include commercially produced videos, examples of management self-development activities, key reference books, exemplar qestionnaires that might be used for needs identification, evaluation, etc.

Provide Advice and Facilitate Networking between Schools

As well as building a resource bank of materials, the LEA (or more specifically the person acting as LEA management development co-ordinator) could usefully build up a databank of information about management trainers, consultants, local-authority personnel, industrialists, etc., who could usefully support management development in school. This would mean, for example, that a school that wanted someone to run a session on team-building or that wanted some information about how selection and appointment procedures were handled in other schools, could fairly quickly be given the name of someone they might turn to for advice.

PART IV
APPENDICES

APPENDIX I
SOME FURTHER READING

Birchenough, M. (1984) *Making School Based Review Work*, NDC, Bristol. An account of the principles and practice of school-based review and development in England and Wales, illustrated by several schemes in use that raise a number of management issues.

Bradley, H. *et al.* (1989) *Report on the Evaluation of the School Teacher Appraisal Pilot Study*, Institute of Education, Cambridge.

Capell, A., Mills, D. and Poster, C. (1987) *Training and Development Needs Questionnaire*, NDC SMT, Bristol.

Department of Education and Science (1987) *School Teachers Pay and Conditions Document*, HMSO, London.

Department of Education and Science (1989) *School Teacher Appraisal: A National Framework. Report of the National Steering Group and the School Teacher Appraisal Pilot Study*, HMSO, London.

Eraut, M., Pennycuick, D. and Radnor, H. (1988) *Local Evaluation of INSET: A Meta-Evaluation of TRIST Evaluations*, Training Agency, 236 Gray's Inn Road, London WC1X 8HL. A report of how LEAs evaluated their INSET programmes during TRIST. It highlights and discusses the important evaluation issues arising from TRIST and makes recommendations for evaluating INSET in the future.

Gane, V. (1987) *Pre-Retirement Preparation for Teachers*, NDC, Bristol. This study surveys current practice in a sample of LEAs, examines some industrial schemes and reviews statistics on teacher retirement. The pre-retirement needs of teachers are identified and practical recommendations are put forward.

ILEA (1988) *Keeping the School under Review*, ILEA Learning Resources Unit, London.

McMahon, A. and Bolam, R. (1990a) *A Handbook for LEAs*, Paul Chapman, London. A practical handbook for LEA advisory services and others involved in managing school management development and training.

McMahon, A. and Bolam, R. (1990a) *A Handbook for Primary Schools*, Paul Chapman, London.

McMahon, A. and Wallace, M. (forthcoming) *School Teacher Appraisal: Primary Handbook*, Paul Chapman, London.

National Steering Group (1988) *Consortium of School Teacher Appraisal Pilot Schemes – Progress on Appraisal: Interim Report*, NDC, Bristol.

Niblett, B. (1986a) *Appraisal: Annotated Bibliography No. 1*, NDC, Bristol. Includes abstracts covering general accounts of experiences with appraisal, job analysis, purpose, principles and techniques, schemes, audio-visual aids and other course material.

Niblett, B. (1986b) *School Management: NDC Annotated Bibliography No. 3*, NDC, Bristol. Includes abstracts of material covering the role and tasks of the head, deputy, head of department and curriculum adviser, a section on management of staff and the management of different kinds of school.

Niblett, B. (1986c) *Training Methods and Materials: NDC Annotated Bibliography No. 2*, NDC, Bristol. Consists of abstracts of materials covering major management training methods such as self-development and problem-solving; materials include manuals, exercises, case studies and audio-visual aids.

Niblett, B. (1986d) *Women and Management: NDC Annotated Bibliography No. 4*, NDC, Bristol. Includes abstracts of materials on training, recruitment, promotion, career breaks, harassment, assertiveness and equal opportunities in education.

Niblett, B. (1987) *Managing INSET: NDC Annotated Bibliography No. 5*, NDC, Bristol. Abstracts include items covering management issues at different levels in the education system, the content of staff development, and the process of needs analysis, programme design, methods and evaluation.

Niblett, B. (1988a) *Appraisal: Supplement to Annotated Bibliography No. 1*, NDC, Bristol. Consists of abstracts of materials covering major management training methods such as self-development and problem-solving; materials include manuals, exercises, case studies and audio-visual aids.

Niblett, B. (1988b) *Managing the Implementation of Educational Reforms: NDC Annotated Bibliography No. 6*, NDC, Bristol. Covers the key innovations covered by the Education Act 1988 and the process of managing change.

Oldroyd, D. and Hall, V. (1988) *Managing Professional Development and INSET: A Handbook for Schools and Colleges*, Training Agency, 236 Gray's Inn Road, London WC1X 8HL. A practical handbook intended for those who have responsibility for managing in-service education at school and college level. Each section examines the relevant management processes and provides examples of how schools and managers tackled them.

Poster, C. and Murphy, M. (1987) *Training and Development Needs Questionnaire: Handbook for Schools*, NDC, Bristol.

Styan, D. (1989) *School Management Task Force: Interim Report* (mimeo 23pp) DES, London.

Wallace, M. (1986) *A Directory of School Management Activities and Resources*, NDC, Bristol. A directory containing an outline of a wide range of activities, many of which may be carried out in school or as part of an external course. Includes a list of resources and advice on choosing, planning and evaluating activities.

Wallace, M. (1988) *School Management Training: Towards a New Partnership*, NDC, Bristol. An overview of current management training practice in England and Wales with a case study on training in Northern Ireland, which raises issues and puts forward recommendations for improving the planning of school management courses and their surrounding processes.

APPENDIX II
ACKNOWLEDGEMENTS

The following are the LEA co-ordination teams and schools who collaborated with the NDC in the management development project.

Birmingham

LEA co-ordination team:	Ken Lambert
	Jean Carter
	Arnold Ingoldsby
Schools:	Broadway School
	Cadbury Sixth Form College
	Hallmoor School
	Small Heath School

Cambridgeshire

LEA co-ordination team:	Colin Curtis
	John Pearce
	Charles Dodd
Schools:	Bassingbourn Village College
	Long Road Sixth Form College
	St Ivo School
	Soham Village College

Cleveland

LEA co-ordination team:	Harold Heller
	Brian Bailey
	Ken Oakley
Schools:	Egglescliffe Secondary
	Newlands
	Rosecroft Secondary
	Bishopsmill Special School

Dorset

LEA co-ordination team:	Peter Mann
	Peter McGargle
	John Farthing

Schools: Allenbourn Middle School
                                   Cranbourne Middle School
                                   Queen Elizabeth's School
                                   Slades Farm School

Gwent

LEA co-ordination team: Russell Cooper
                                   Ian Lewis
                                   Jeff Portch
Schools: Llantarnam Comprehensive School
                                   Nantyglo Comprehensive School
                                   Oakdale Comprehensive School
                                   Castle Hill School

Leeds

LEA co-ordination team: Stuart Johnson
                                   Margaret McIntosh
                                   John West
                                   Arthur Harvey
Schools: Armley Middle School
                                   Broomfield School
                                   Guiseley School
                                   Stainbeck High School
                                   Whinmoor Middle School

Northamptonshire

LEA co-ordination team: Roger Martin
                                   Dan Dingle
                                   Bill Shaw
                                   George Gyte
Schools: Chenderit School
                                   Eastfield Park School
                                   Ecton Brook Middle School
                                   Montsaye School

South Glamorgan

LEA co-ordination team: Derrick Orrell
                                   Ivor Evenden
                                   Eddie Roberts
Schools: Fitzalan High School
                                   Glyn Derw High School
                                   Meadowbank School
                                   Whitchurch High School

INDEX